50 Persian Entree Recipes for Home

By: Kelly Johnson

Table of Contents

- Fesenjan (Pomegranate Walnut Stew)
- Ghormeh Sabzi (Herb Stew with Meat and Kidney Beans)
- Zereshk Polo Ba Morgh (Barberry Rice with Chicken)
- Baghali Polo (Dill and Lima Bean Rice)
- Khoresht Gheymeh (Split Pea Stew with Meat)
- Tahchin (Saffron Rice Cake with Chicken)
- Joojeh Kabab (Grilled Saffron Chicken Kebabs)
- Adas Polo (Lentil Rice)
- Koofteh Tabrizi (Stuffed Meatballs from Tabriz)
- Sabzi Polo Ba Mahi (Herb Rice with Fish)
- Abgoosht (Persian Lamb and Chickpea Stew)
- Dolmeh Barg (Stuffed Grape Leaves with Meat)
- Ashe Reshteh (Noodle and Herb Soup)
- Chelo Kebab Koobideh (Grilled Ground Meat Kebabs)
- Morgh Polo (Chicken and Rice)
- Khoresh Bademjan (Eggplant Stew with Meat)
- Mast O Khiar (Yogurt with Cucumber and Mint)
- Kuku Sabzi (Herb Frittata)
- Chelo Morgh (Saffron Chicken and Rice)
- Baghali Ghatogh (Lima Bean and Dill Stew)
- Khoresh Karafs (Celery Stew with Meat)
- Ash-e Doogh (Yogurt Soup)
- Shishlik (Grilled Lamb Skewers)
- Kalam Polo (Cabbage Rice)
- Mirza Ghasemi (Smoked Eggplant and Tomato Dip)
- Saffron Chicken and Barberry Rice
- Khoresh Mast (Yogurt Stew with Meat)
- Gondi (Chickpea and Chicken Dumplings)
- Lubia Polo (Green Bean Rice)
- Khoresh-e Nokhod (Chickpea Stew)
- Tahdig with Chicken (Crispy Rice with Chicken)
- Khoresh Bamieh (Okra Stew with Meat)
- Baqlava (Persian Walnut Pastry)
- Mirza Qasemi (Eggplant and Tomato Dip)
- Khoresh-e Albaloo (Sour Cherry Stew with Meat)

- Maast-o Esfenaj (Yogurt with Spinach)
- Kabab Torsh (Sour Chicken Kebabs)
- Khoresh-e Beh (Quince Stew with Meat)
- Ash-e Anar (Pomegranate Soup)
- Persian Herb Omelette (Omlet-e Sabzi)
- Khoresh-e Havij (Carrot Stew with Meat)
- Mahicheh Stew (Lamb Shank Stew)
- Gheymeh Nesar (Lentil and Dried Lime Stew)
- Persian Rice Pilaf with Pistachios and Dill
- Khoresh-e Karafs (Celery Stew with Meat)
- Kotlet (Persian Meat Patties)
- Sabzi Khordan (Fresh Herb Platter)
- Khoresh-e Fesenjan (Pomegranate Walnut Stew with Chicken)
- Sirabi Polo (Cherry Rice)
- Ash-e Reshteh (Noodle and Herb Soup)

Fesenjan (Pomegranate Walnut Stew)

Ingredients:

- 1 cup walnuts, finely ground
- 1 large onion, finely chopped
- 2 tablespoons vegetable oil
- 500g boneless chicken thighs, cut into bite-sized pieces (or duck if preferred)
- 1 cup pomegranate molasses
- 1 tablespoon sugar (optional, adjust to taste)
- 1/2 teaspoon ground cinnamon
- Salt and pepper to taste
- Pomegranate seeds for garnish (optional)

Instructions:

Prepare Walnuts:
- In a food processor, grind the walnuts until they form a fine powder. Be careful not to over-process, as you don't want to end up with walnut butter.

Sauté Onion:
- In a large pot, heat vegetable oil over medium heat. Sauté the finely chopped onion until it becomes golden brown.

Cook Chicken:
- Add the chicken pieces to the pot and brown them on all sides.

Add Ground Walnuts:
- Once the chicken is browned, add the ground walnuts to the pot. Stir well to coat the chicken in the ground walnuts.

Pomegranate Molasses and Spices:
- Pour in the pomegranate molasses, and add sugar (if using), ground cinnamon, salt, and pepper. Mix everything together.

Simmer:
- Reduce the heat to low, cover the pot, and let the stew simmer for about 1 to 1.5 hours, or until the chicken is tender and the flavors have melded. Stir occasionally.

Adjust Seasoning:
- Taste the stew and adjust the seasoning according to your preferences. You can add more salt, pepper, or sugar if needed.

Garnish and Serve:

- Once the stew has reached the desired consistency, and the chicken is tender, it's ready to be served.
- Optionally, garnish with pomegranate seeds for a burst of freshness and color.

Serve with Rice:
- Fesenjan is traditionally served with Persian rice. Prepare your favorite rice dish to accompany the stew.

Enjoy:
- Serve Fesenjan in a bowl over rice and savor the unique combination of sweet and savory flavors.

Fesenjan is a delightful dish with a perfect balance of tanginess from pomegranate molasses and richness from ground walnuts. It's a true celebration of Persian flavors.

Ghormeh Sabzi (Herb Stew with Meat and Kidney Beans)

Ingredients:

- 1 cup dried kidney beans, soaked overnight (or canned kidney beans, drained)
- 500g lamb or beef stew meat, cut into bite-sized pieces
- 2 cups chopped fresh herbs (a mix of parsley, cilantro, and green onions)
- 1 cup chopped fenugreek leaves (optional)
- 1 large onion, finely chopped
- 4 cloves garlic, minced
- 1 teaspoon ground turmeric
- 1 teaspoon ground cinnamon
- Salt and pepper to taste
- 1/2 cup vegetable oil
- 2 dried limes (limoo amani), pierced (optional)
- 1 tablespoon dried fenugreek leaves (kasuri methi), crushed (optional)
- 1 cup water
- Juice of 1-2 limes or lemons
- Steamed rice for serving

Instructions:

Prepare Kidney Beans:
- If using dried kidney beans, soak them overnight. Drain and rinse. Boil in water until tender. If using canned kidney beans, drain and rinse.

Sauté Onions and Meat:
- In a large pot, heat vegetable oil over medium heat. Sauté chopped onions until golden brown.
- Add the meat pieces to the pot. Brown the meat on all sides.

Add Aromatics and Spices:
- Stir in minced garlic, ground turmeric, ground cinnamon, salt, and pepper. Mix well.

Incorporate Fresh Herbs:
- Add the chopped fresh herbs (parsley, cilantro, green onions) to the pot. If available, include chopped fenugreek leaves for an extra layer of flavor.

Cook Herbs:
- Cook the herbs with the meat and aromatics until they are wilted and release their fragrance.

Add Kidney Beans:
- Incorporate the cooked or canned kidney beans into the pot. Mix well.

Dried Limes and Fenugreek Leaves (Optional):
- If using dried limes, pierce them with a knife and add them to the pot. Also, add crushed dried fenugreek leaves for additional flavor.

Add Water and Simmer:
- Pour in the water and bring the stew to a boil. Reduce the heat to low, cover the pot, and let it simmer for about 2 to 2.5 hours, or until the meat is tender and the flavors are well combined. Stir occasionally.

Adjust Seasoning:
- Taste the stew and adjust the seasoning. If you prefer a more tangy flavor, add lime or lemon juice.

Serve:
- Ghormeh Sabzi is traditionally served with steamed rice.

Enjoy:
- Ladle the stew over rice and enjoy the delicious blend of herbs, spices, and tender meat.

Ghormeh Sabzi is a cherished dish in Persian cuisine, and its unique combination of herbs and spices makes it a flavorful and comforting stew.

Zereshk Polo Ba Morgh (Barberry Rice with Chicken)

Ingredients:

For the Chicken:

- 500g chicken pieces (thighs, drumsticks, or a whole chicken, cut into parts)
- 1 large onion, finely chopped
- 2 tablespoons vegetable oil
- 1 teaspoon ground turmeric
- Salt and pepper to taste

For the Barberry Rice:

- 2 cups Basmati rice, rinsed and soaked
- 1 cup dried barberries (zereshk)
- 3 tablespoons butter or ghee
- 1/2 teaspoon ground saffron threads (soaked in warm water)
- 1/4 cup sugar
- Salt to taste

Optional Garnish:

- Sliced almonds or slivered pistachios

Instructions:

Prepare Chicken:
- In a pot, heat vegetable oil over medium heat. Sauté chopped onions until golden brown.
- Add chicken pieces to the pot. Season with ground turmeric, salt, and pepper. Brown the chicken on all sides.
- Add a bit of water to the pot, cover, and let the chicken cook over medium-low heat until fully cooked. Ensure the chicken is tender and flavorful. Remove from heat and set aside.

Prepare Barberries:
- Rinse the dried barberries in cold water to remove any impurities.
- In a small pan, melt 1 tablespoon of butter or ghee. Add the barberries and sauté for a few minutes. Sprinkle sugar over the barberries and continue to sauté until they become plump and slightly caramelized. Set aside.

Cook Rice:
- In a large pot, bring water to a boil. Add salt and the soaked Basmati rice. Cook until the rice is parboiled (half-cooked). Drain the rice.
- In the same pot, melt the remaining butter or ghee. Place a layer of parboiled rice at the bottom.

Layer Rice and Barberries:
- Add a layer of rice on top of the butter, then sprinkle half of the sautéed barberries over the rice.
- Repeat the layering process, finishing with a layer of rice on top. Pour the saffron-infused water over the rice.

Steam the Rice:
- Cover the pot with a clean kitchen towel and a tight-fitting lid. Cook on low heat for about 1 to 1.5 hours to allow the rice to steam and fully cook.

Serve:
- Once the rice is fully cooked, gently fluff it with a fork.
- Place the rice on a serving platter, and arrange the cooked chicken pieces on top. Garnish with the remaining barberries and, if desired, sliced almonds or slivered pistachios.

Enjoy:
- Zereshk Polo Ba Morgh is ready to be enjoyed. Serve this flavorful dish with the chicken on a bed of beautifully layered and saffron-infused rice.

Zereshk Polo Ba Morgh is a festive and aromatic dish, perfect for special occasions and celebrations in Persian cuisine.

Baghali Polo (Dill and Lima Bean Rice)

Ingredients:

- 2 cups Basmati rice, rinsed and soaked
- 1 cup fresh or frozen lima beans (baghali), thawed if frozen
- 1 cup fresh dill, chopped
- 1 large onion, finely chopped
- 3 tablespoons vegetable oil or ghee
- 1 teaspoon ground saffron threads (soaked in warm water)
- Salt and pepper to taste

Instructions:

Prepare Rice:
- In a large pot, bring water to a boil. Add salt and the soaked Basmati rice. Cook until the rice is parboiled (half-cooked). Drain the rice.
- In the same pot, heat vegetable oil or ghee. Place a layer of parboiled rice at the bottom.

Prepare Lima Beans and Dill:
- In a separate pan, sauté the chopped onions in a bit of oil until golden brown.
- Add lima beans to the pan and cook until they are slightly tender.
- Stir in chopped fresh dill and cook for a few more minutes until the dill is wilted.

Layer Rice and Lima Bean-Dill Mixture:
- Add a layer of rice on top of the oil in the pot, followed by a layer of the lima bean-dill mixture. Repeat until all the rice and the mixture are used.

Saffron Infusion:
- Sprinkle the saffron-infused water over the top layer of rice.

Steam the Rice:
- Cover the pot with a clean kitchen towel and a tight-fitting lid. Cook on low heat for about 1 to 1.5 hours to allow the rice to steam and fully cook.

Serve:
- Once the rice is fully cooked, gently fluff it with a fork to mix the layers.
- Transfer the Baghali Polo to a serving platter, ensuring that the lima bean-dill mixture is distributed throughout the rice.

Enjoy:

- Baghali Polo is ready to be enjoyed. Serve it as a flavorful side dish alongside your favorite Persian main courses.

This Baghali Polo recipe captures the essence of Persian cuisine with the aromatic combination of dill and lima beans, making it a delightful addition to any meal.

Khoresht Gheymeh (Split Pea Stew with Meat)

Ingredients:

- 1 cup yellow split peas, rinsed
- 500g beef or lamb stew meat, cut into bite-sized pieces
- 1 large onion, finely chopped
- 3 tablespoons vegetable oil
- 1 teaspoon turmeric
- Salt and pepper to taste
- 2 dried limes (limoo amani), pierced
- 2 tablespoons tomato paste
- 1 tablespoon dried fenugreek leaves (optional)
- 1 large potato, peeled and cut into small cubes
- Water or beef broth
- 1 tablespoon lime or lemon juice
- Saffron threads (optional, for garnish)
- Fried onions or crispy potato strips (for garnish)
- Steamed rice for serving

Instructions:

Prepare Split Peas:
- Rinse the yellow split peas thoroughly and soak them in water for at least 1-2 hours.

Sauté Onions and Meat:
- In a large pot, heat vegetable oil over medium heat. Sauté chopped onions until golden brown.
- Add the stew meat to the pot. Season with turmeric, salt, and pepper. Brown the meat on all sides.

Add Tomato Paste and Dried Lime:
- Stir in tomato paste and cook for a couple of minutes.
- Add the pierced dried limes to the pot, along with fenugreek leaves if using. Mix well.

Cook Split Peas:
- Drain the soaked split peas and add them to the pot. Stir to combine with the meat and other ingredients.

- Pour in enough water or beef broth to cover the ingredients. Bring the stew to a boil, then reduce the heat to low, cover the pot, and let it simmer for about 1.5 to 2 hours or until the meat and split peas are tender.

Add Potatoes:
- Add the cubed potatoes to the pot and continue simmering until the potatoes are cooked through and the stew reaches the desired consistency.

Adjust Seasoning:
- Taste the stew and adjust the seasoning if needed. If you prefer a hint of acidity, add lime or lemon juice.

Garnish and Serve:
- Optionally, garnish the Khoresht Gheymeh with saffron threads for color.
- Serve the stew over steamed rice and garnish with fried onions or crispy potato strips.

Enjoy:
- Khoresht Gheymeh is ready to be enjoyed, offering a delightful combination of flavors and textures.

This Persian split pea stew is a comforting and hearty dish that is often enjoyed with rice, creating a satisfying and flavorful meal.

Tahchin (Saffron Rice Cake with Chicken)

Ingredients:

For the Rice Layer:

- 2 cups Basmati rice, rinsed and soaked
- 2 cups plain yogurt
- 2 large eggs
- 1/2 cup vegetable oil
- 1 teaspoon ground saffron threads (soaked in warm water)
- Salt and pepper to taste

For the Chicken Layer:

- 500g chicken thighs or breasts, cooked and shredded
- 1 large onion, finely chopped
- 2 tablespoons vegetable oil
- 1 teaspoon ground turmeric
- Salt and pepper to taste

For Garnish:

- Saffron threads (optional, for garnish)
- Slivered almonds or pistachios (optional)

Instructions:

Prepare Rice:
- In a large pot, bring water to a boil. Add salt and the soaked Basmati rice. Cook until the rice is parboiled (half-cooked). Drain the rice.
- In a mixing bowl, combine the parboiled rice, yogurt, eggs, vegetable oil, saffron-infused water, salt, and pepper. Mix well to form a thick batter.

Prepare Chicken:
- In a pan, heat vegetable oil over medium heat. Sauté chopped onions until golden brown.
- Add shredded cooked chicken to the pan. Season with ground turmeric, salt, and pepper. Stir well to coat the chicken with the spices. Cook for a few minutes until the chicken is infused with flavors.

Layering:

- Preheat the oven to 350°F (180°C).
- Grease a round or rectangular baking dish. Pour half of the rice batter into the dish and spread it evenly to form the first layer.
- Add the seasoned and cooked chicken over the rice layer, creating an even second layer.
- Cover the chicken layer with the remaining rice batter, spreading it evenly to form the top layer.

Bake:
- Cover the baking dish with aluminum foil. Bake in the preheated oven for about 1 to 1.5 hours, or until the rice forms a golden crust and is fully cooked.

Cool and Invert:
- Allow the Tahchin to cool slightly. To serve, invert the baking dish onto a serving platter, revealing the beautiful layers.

Garnish:
- Garnish the Tahchin with saffron threads and slivered almonds or pistachios for an extra touch of flavor and decoration.

Slice and Serve:
- Slice the Tahchin into wedges or squares. Serve it warm as a main dish or a festive side dish.

Enjoy:
- Tahchin is ready to be enjoyed, offering a delightful combination of crispy rice layers and flavorful chicken.

Tahchin is a festive and visually stunning dish that brings the flavors of saffron-infused rice and seasoned chicken together in a unique and delightful way.

Joojeh Kabab (Grilled Saffron Chicken Kebabs)

Ingredients:

For the Marinade:

- 500g boneless, skinless chicken thighs, cut into bite-sized pieces
- 1 large onion, grated
- 1/2 cup plain yogurt
- 2 tablespoons olive oil
- 2 tablespoons lemon juice
- 2 cloves garlic, minced
- 1 teaspoon ground saffron threads (soaked in warm water)
- 1 teaspoon ground turmeric
- Salt and pepper to taste

For the Kebabs:

- Skewers, wooden or metal
- Cherry tomatoes (optional, for skewering with chicken)

Instructions:

Prepare the Marinade:
- In a bowl, combine grated onion, plain yogurt, olive oil, lemon juice, minced garlic, soaked saffron, ground turmeric, salt, and pepper. Mix well to form the marinade.

Marinate the Chicken:
- Place the chicken pieces in the marinade, ensuring they are well coated. Cover the bowl and let the chicken marinate for at least 4 hours, or preferably overnight in the refrigerator.

Skewer the Chicken:
- If using wooden skewers, soak them in water for about 30 minutes to prevent burning during grilling.
- Skewer the marinated chicken pieces onto the skewers, and if desired, alternate with cherry tomatoes.

Grill the Kebabs:
- Preheat the grill to medium-high heat. Brush the grates with oil to prevent sticking.

- Grill the Joojeh Kababs for about 10-15 minutes, turning occasionally, until the chicken is fully cooked and has a nice char.

Serve:
- Once the Joojeh Kababs are cooked, transfer them to a serving platter.

Garnish (Optional):
- Garnish with additional saffron threads for color.

Enjoy:
- Joojeh Kabab is ready to be enjoyed! Serve the grilled saffron chicken kebabs with rice, flatbread, or your favorite Persian side dishes.

This Joojeh Kabab recipe delivers tender and flavorful grilled chicken with the unique aroma and color of saffron. It's a wonderful dish for gatherings and celebrations, bringing the essence of Persian cuisine to your table.

Adas Polo (Lentil Rice)

Ingredients:

- 1 cup Basmati rice, rinsed and soaked
- 1 cup lentils, rinsed and soaked
- 1 large onion, finely chopped
- 3 tablespoons vegetable oil or ghee
- 1 teaspoon ground cinnamon
- 1 teaspoon ground cumin
- 1/2 teaspoon ground turmeric
- Salt and pepper to taste
- 1/2 cup raisins or barberries (zereshk), soaked (optional for garnish)
- Saffron threads, soaked in warm water (optional for coloring)
- Slivered almonds or chopped pistachios (optional for garnish)

Instructions:

Prepare Lentils:
- Rinse and soak the lentils in water for about 1-2 hours.

Cook Rice:
- In a large pot, bring water to a boil. Add salt and the soaked Basmati rice. Cook until the rice is parboiled (half-cooked). Drain the rice.

Sauté Onions and Lentils:
- In a pan, heat vegetable oil or ghee over medium heat. Sauté chopped onions until golden brown.
- Add the soaked and drained lentils to the pan. Stir in ground cinnamon, ground cumin, ground turmeric, salt, and pepper. Cook until the lentils are tender.

Layer Rice and Lentils:
- In the same pot used for the rice, layer the parboiled rice with the cooked lentils and onions. Create alternating layers, starting and ending with a layer of rice.

Saffron Infusion (Optional):
- If using saffron, sprinkle the saffron-infused water over the top layer of rice to create a yellow color.

Steam the Rice:

- Cover the pot with a clean kitchen towel and a tight-fitting lid. Cook on low heat for about 1 to 1.5 hours to allow the rice to steam and fully cook.

Garnish (Optional):
- If desired, garnish Adas Polo with soaked raisins or barberries, and slivered almonds or chopped pistachios.

Serve:
- Once the rice is fully cooked, gently fluff it with a fork, mixing the layers.
- Transfer Adas Polo to a serving platter.

Enjoy:
- Adas Polo is ready to be enjoyed as a flavorful and comforting dish. Serve it as a side or a main course.

This Persian lentil rice dish showcases a delightful blend of spices and textures, making it a wonderful addition to your repertoire of Persian recipes.

Koofteh Tabrizi (Stuffed Meatballs from Tabriz)

Ingredients:

For the Meatballs:

- 500g ground beef or lamb
- 1 cup cooked rice
- 1 large onion, grated
- 2 eggs
- 1/2 cup chickpea flour (besan)
- 1 teaspoon ground turmeric
- Salt and pepper to taste
- 1 teaspoon baking soda

For the Filling:

- 200g ground beef or lamb
- 1 large onion, finely chopped
- 1/2 cup cooked split peas
- 1/4 cup chopped fresh herbs (parsley, cilantro, mint)
- 1 teaspoon ground cinnamon
- Salt and pepper to taste

For the Sauce:

- 2 tablespoons tomato paste
- 1 tablespoon dried mint
- 1 teaspoon ground turmeric
- 1 tablespoon vegetable oil
- Salt and pepper to taste

Instructions:

Prepare the Meatball Mixture:
- In a large bowl, combine ground meat, cooked rice, grated onion, eggs, chickpea flour, ground turmeric, salt, pepper, and baking soda. Mix well until all ingredients are thoroughly combined.

Prepare the Filling:

- In a separate bowl, mix together ground meat, finely chopped onion, cooked split peas, chopped fresh herbs, ground cinnamon, salt, and pepper.

Assemble the Meatballs:
- Take a handful of the meatball mixture and flatten it in your palm. Place a portion of the filling in the center and enclose it with the meat mixture, forming a large stuffed meatball.

Cook the Meatballs:
- In a large pot, bring water to a boil. Gently place the stuffed meatballs into the boiling water and let them simmer for about 30-40 minutes or until they are fully cooked. Ensure the meatballs are not too crowded in the pot.

Prepare the Sauce:
- In a separate pan, mix together tomato paste, dried mint, ground turmeric, vegetable oil, salt, and pepper. Cook the sauce over low heat for about 10 minutes.

Serve:
- Carefully transfer the cooked stuffed meatballs to a serving dish.
- Pour the prepared sauce over the meatballs, ensuring they are well coated.

Enjoy:
- Koofteh Tabrizi is ready to be enjoyed! Serve it with flatbread, rice, or on its own.

This flavorful and hearty dish showcases the culinary richness of Iranian cuisine, and Koofteh Tabrizi is sure to be a delightful addition to your Persian recipe collection.

Sabzi Polo Ba Mahi (Herb Rice with Fish)

Ingredients:

For the Herb Rice (Sabzi Polo):

- 2 cups Basmati rice, rinsed and soaked
- 1 cup chopped fresh herbs (a combination of dill, parsley, cilantro, green onions)
- 2 cloves garlic, minced
- 1/2 cup vegetable oil or ghee
- Salt and pepper to taste
- 1 teaspoon ground saffron threads (soaked in warm water)

For the Fish:

- 4 fillets of white fish (such as cod or tilapia)
- Juice of 1 lemon
- 2 tablespoons olive oil
- Salt and pepper to taste
- Optional: Sumac for garnish

Instructions:

Prepare Herb Rice (Sabzi Polo):
- In a pot, bring water to a boil. Add salt and the soaked Basmati rice. Cook until the rice is parboiled (half-cooked). Drain the rice.
- In a large mixing bowl, combine the parboiled rice with chopped fresh herbs, minced garlic, vegetable oil or ghee, salt, and pepper. Mix well to evenly distribute the herbs.
- In the same pot used for the rice, create alternating layers of rice and herb mixture. Finish with a layer of rice on top.
- Sprinkle the saffron-infused water over the top layer of rice.
- Cover the pot with a clean kitchen towel and a tight-fitting lid. Cook on low heat for about 1 to 1.5 hours to allow the rice to steam and fully cook.

Prepare the Fish:
- Marinate the fish fillets in lemon juice, olive oil, salt, and pepper for about 15-30 minutes.
- Grill or pan-fry the fish fillets until they are cooked through and have a nice golden color.

Serve:

- Once the rice is fully cooked, gently fluff it with a fork to mix the layers.
- Place the Sabzi Polo on a serving platter, and arrange the grilled or pan-fried fish fillets on top.
- Optional: Garnish with a sprinkle of sumac for extra flavor and color.

Enjoy:
- Sabzi Polo Ba Mahi is ready to be enjoyed! Serve this flavorful dish with a side of yogurt or your favorite Persian condiments.

This Persian herb rice with fish is a festive and aromatic dish, perfect for special occasions and celebrations in Iranian cuisine.

Abgoosht (Persian Lamb and Chickpea Stew)

Ingredients:

For the Stew:

- 1.5 pounds lamb stew meat, cut into chunks
- 1 cup chickpeas, soaked overnight
- 2 large onions, chopped
- 2 large tomatoes, chopped
- 3 medium potatoes, peeled and quartered
- 3 carrots, peeled and cut into chunks
- 2-3 cloves garlic, minced
- 1 teaspoon turmeric
- 1 teaspoon ground cumin
- Salt and pepper to taste
- 1 tablespoon tomato paste
- 6 cups water

For the Garnish:

- 1 bunch fresh mint, chopped
- 1 bunch fresh cilantro, chopped
- 1 bunch green onions, chopped
- Radishes, sliced
- 1 lime, cut into wedges
- Flatbread or Sangak (Persian flatbread)

Instructions:

Prepare Chickpeas:
- If using dried chickpeas, soak them overnight in water. Drain before using.

Sauté Onions and Garlic:
- In a large pot, sauté chopped onions in oil until golden brown. Add minced garlic and sauté for an additional minute.

Brown Lamb and Add Spices:
- Add lamb chunks to the pot and brown them on all sides. Sprinkle turmeric, ground cumin, salt, and pepper over the meat.

Add Vegetables and Chickpeas:

- Add chopped tomatoes, tomato paste, soaked chickpeas, potatoes, and carrots to the pot. Mix well.

Pour Water and Simmer:
- Pour water over the ingredients in the pot, ensuring they are fully covered. Bring the stew to a boil, then reduce the heat to low. Cover the pot and let it simmer for about 2-3 hours or until the meat is tender and the flavors meld.

Separate Broth and Solids:
- Once cooked, separate the broth from the solids using a slotted spoon. Mash the solids with a potato masher or the back of a ladle to create a coarse mixture.

Serve:
- Serve Abgoosht by placing the mashed solids on a plate or in a bowl. Pour some of the broth over the mashed mixture.

Garnish:
- Garnish the stew with chopped mint, cilantro, and green onions. Serve with sliced radishes and lime wedges on the side.

Enjoy:
- Abgoosht is traditionally eaten by tearing pieces of flatbread and dipping them into the stew. Squeeze lime juice over the stew for added flavor.

This traditional Persian lamb and chickpea stew is a comforting and communal dish that is enjoyed with family and friends, making it a significant part of Iranian culinary culture.

Dolmeh Barg (Stuffed Grape Leaves with Meat)

Ingredients:

For the Filling:

- 1 cup Basmati rice, rinsed and soaked
- 300g ground beef or lamb
- 1 large onion, finely chopped
- 1/2 cup finely chopped fresh herbs (a mix of dill, parsley, and mint)
- 1/4 cup pine nuts (optional)
- 1 teaspoon ground cinnamon
- Salt and pepper to taste

For the Grape Leaves:

- 1 jar of grape leaves in brine (about 60-70 leaves)
- Juice of 2 lemons
- 2 tablespoons olive oil

For Cooking:

- Water or vegetable broth
- 2-3 cloves garlic, minced
- 2 tablespoons tomato paste
- Salt and pepper to taste

Instructions:

Prepare the Grape Leaves:
- Rinse the grape leaves under cold water to remove excess brine. Place them in a bowl and cover with boiling water for about 10-15 minutes to soften. Drain and set aside.

Prepare the Filling:
- In a bowl, mix together soaked Basmati rice, ground beef or lamb, finely chopped onion, chopped fresh herbs, pine nuts (if using), ground cinnamon, salt, and pepper. Ensure the mixture is well combined.

Fill the Grape Leaves:
- Lay a grape leaf flat with the shiny side down. Place a tablespoon of the filling near the stem end of the leaf.

- Fold the sides of the leaf over the filling and roll from the stem end towards the tip, creating a cigar-like shape. Repeat with the remaining grape leaves and filling.

Cooking the Dolmeh:
- In a large pot, spread a layer of grape leaves on the bottom to prevent sticking.
- Arrange the stuffed grape leaves in layers in the pot, packing them tightly.
- Mix minced garlic, tomato paste, and olive oil with water or vegetable broth. Pour this mixture over the stuffed grape leaves.
- Place a heavy plate upside down on top of the dolmeh to keep them in place during cooking.
- Cover the pot and simmer over low heat for about 1.5 to 2 hours, or until the rice is fully cooked.

Serve:
- Once cooked, carefully remove the stuffed grape leaves from the pot and arrange them on a serving platter.
- Optionally, drizzle with lemon juice and olive oil before serving.

Enjoy:
- Dolmeh Barg is ready to be enjoyed! Serve it as an appetizer or part of a larger Persian meal.

This Dolmeh Barg recipe offers a delightful combination of flavors and textures, showcasing the rich tradition of Persian stuffed grape leaves.

Ashe Reshteh (Noodle and Herb Soup)

Ingredients:

For the Soup Base:

- 1 cup lentils, rinsed
- 1 cup chickpeas, soaked overnight
- 1 cup red kidney beans, soaked overnight
- 1 large onion, chopped
- 4 cloves garlic, minced
- 1/2 cup vegetable oil
- 1/2 teaspoon turmeric
- Salt and pepper to taste

For the Herbs and Noodles:

- 2 cups chopped fresh herbs (a mix of parsley, cilantro, green onions, spinach)
- 200g reshteh (Persian flat noodles) or linguine, broken into small pieces
- 1/2 cup chopped spinach
- 1/2 cup chopped dill
- 1/2 cup chopped cilantro

For Garnish:

- 1 tablespoon dried mint, fried in oil until crispy
- 1/2 cup kashk (whey, optional)
- 1 large onion, thinly sliced and fried until golden
- 2 tablespoons vinegar
- 2 tablespoons olive oil

Instructions:

Prepare the Legumes:
- In a large pot, combine lentils, soaked chickpeas, and red kidney beans. Cover with water and bring to a boil. Simmer until the legumes are tender.

Sauté Onions and Garlic:
- In a separate pan, sauté chopped onions and minced garlic in vegetable oil until golden brown.
- Add turmeric, salt, and pepper to the onion and garlic mixture. Stir well.

Combine Soup Base and Herbs:

- Add the sautéed onion and garlic mixture to the pot with the cooked legumes.
- Add chopped fresh herbs, spinach, dill, and cilantro to the pot. Allow the soup to simmer.

Cook Noodles:
- In a separate pot, cook the reshteh or linguine according to package instructions. Drain and add the noodles to the soup.

Simmer:
- Let the soup simmer for an additional 30-40 minutes until the flavors are well combined, and the herbs are fully cooked.

Garnish:
- In a small pan, fry dried mint in oil until crispy.
- In a separate pan, fry thinly sliced onions until golden brown.
- Optional: Mix kashk with vinegar and set aside.

Serve:
- Ladle the Ashe Reshteh into bowls.
- Garnish each serving with fried mint, fried onions, a drizzle of olive oil, and a dollop of kashk if using.

Enjoy:
- Ashe Reshteh is ready to be enjoyed! Serve it hot as a nourishing and flavorful Persian soup.

This Ashe Reshteh recipe captures the essence of Persian cuisine with its rich blend of herbs, legumes, and noodles. It's a delightful dish that is both comforting and celebratory.

Chelo Kebab Koobideh (Grilled Ground Meat Kebabs)

Ingredients:

For the Kebabs:

- 500g ground beef or lamb (a mix of both is common)
- 1 large onion, grated
- 1 egg
- 1 tablespoon sumac
- 1 teaspoon turmeric
- Salt and pepper to taste
- Skewers (metal or soaked wooden skewers)

For Serving:

- Persian rice (chelo)
- Grilled tomatoes
- Sumac (for sprinkling)
- Lavash or flatbread (optional)

Instructions:

Prepare the Meat Mixture:
- In a large bowl, combine ground meat, grated onion, egg, sumac, turmeric, salt, and pepper.
- Mix the ingredients well until everything is evenly incorporated.

Shape the Kebabs:
- Take a portion of the meat mixture and mold it onto the skewer, shaping it into a long, cylindrical kebab. Repeat for the remaining mixture.
- You can wet your hands with water to prevent the meat from sticking.

Grill the Kebabs:
- Preheat a grill or grill pan over medium-high heat.
- Place the kebabs on the grill and cook for about 10-15 minutes, turning occasionally, until they are fully cooked and have a nice char.

Prepare Persian Rice (Chelo):
- Cook Persian rice according to your preferred method. The rice can be steamed or parboiled and then steamed to achieve a fluffy texture.

Serve:

- Arrange the Chelo Kebab Koobideh on a serving platter.
- Place grilled tomatoes alongside the kebabs.
- Optionally, sprinkle sumac over the kebabs for extra flavor.
- Serve with Persian rice and lavash or flatbread if desired.

Enjoy:

- Chelo Kebab Koobideh is ready to be enjoyed! Traditionally, it's eaten by wrapping the kebab in flatbread along with rice and grilled tomatoes.

This recipe captures the essence of Iranian cuisine, offering a flavorful and satisfying dish that is perfect for gatherings and celebrations.

Morgh Polo (Chicken and Rice)

Ingredients:

For the Chicken Marinade:

- 1.5 kg chicken pieces (legs, thighs, or a whole chicken)
- 1 cup plain yogurt
- Juice of 1 lemon
- 2 cloves garlic, minced
- 1 teaspoon ground saffron threads (soaked in warm water)
- Salt and pepper to taste

For the Rice:

- 2 cups Basmati rice, rinsed and soaked
- 1 large onion, thinly sliced
- 1/2 cup vegetable oil or ghee
- 1/2 teaspoon ground saffron threads (soaked in warm water)
- 1/4 cup barberries (zereshk), soaked in water (for garnish)
- Salt and pepper to taste

For Garnish:

- Sliced almonds or slivered pistachios (optional)

Instructions:

Marinate the Chicken:
- In a bowl, mix together yogurt, lemon juice, minced garlic, saffron (soaked in warm water), salt, and pepper to create the marinade.
- Coat the chicken pieces with the marinade, ensuring they are well-covered. Allow it to marinate for at least 2 hours, or overnight in the refrigerator for better flavor.

Prepare the Rice:
- In a pot, bring water to a boil. Add salt and the soaked Basmati rice. Cook until the rice is parboiled (half-cooked). Drain the rice.
- In a separate pan, sauté thinly sliced onions in vegetable oil or ghee until golden brown.
- Mix a portion of the sautéed onions with ground saffron.

- In the pot, layer the parboiled rice with the remaining sautéed onions. Drizzle the saffron-onion mixture over the top layer.
- Cover the pot with a clean kitchen towel and a tight-fitting lid. Cook on low heat for about 1.5 to 2 hours to allow the rice to steam and fully cook.

Grill the Chicken:
- Preheat a grill or oven. Grill or roast the marinated chicken until it's fully cooked and has a nice golden color.

Garnish:
- In a pan, sauté the soaked barberries in a bit of oil until they puff up.
- Optionally, toast sliced almonds or slivered pistachios for garnish.

Serve:
- Once the rice is fully cooked, gently fluff it with a fork, mixing the layers.
- Arrange the Morgh Polo on a serving platter. Place the grilled chicken on top of the rice.
- Garnish with sautéed barberries and toasted almonds or pistachios.

Enjoy:
- Morgh Polo is ready to be enjoyed! Serve it with a side of yogurt or a simple salad.

This Morgh Polo recipe captures the essence of Persian cuisine, offering a delightful combination of saffron-infused rice and flavorful grilled chicken.

Khoresh Bademjan (Eggplant Stew with Meat)

Ingredients:

- 500g lamb or beef stew meat, cut into cubes
- 2 large eggplants, peeled and sliced
- 2 onions, finely chopped
- 4 tomatoes, peeled and chopped (or 1 can of diced tomatoes)
- 3 cloves garlic, minced
- 1 teaspoon turmeric
- 1 teaspoon ground cinnamon
- Salt and pepper to taste
- 1/2 cup vegetable oil
- 1 tablespoon tomato paste
- 1 cup water or beef broth
- Fresh lime or lemon juice (optional, for serving)
- Chopped fresh parsley for garnish

Instructions:

Prepare the Eggplants:
- Peel the eggplants and cut them into thick slices. Sprinkle salt on the slices and let them sit for about 30 minutes to draw out any bitterness. Rinse and pat them dry.
- In a pan, heat some vegetable oil over medium heat. Fry the eggplant slices until they are golden brown on both sides. Set aside on paper towels to drain excess oil.

Sauté Onions and Garlic:
- In a large pot, heat the remaining vegetable oil over medium heat. Add chopped onions and sauté until they become translucent.
- Add minced garlic to the onions and continue sautéing for a couple of minutes until fragrant.

Brown the Meat:
- Add the cubed meat to the pot. Brown the meat on all sides to seal in the flavors.

Add Spices and Tomatoes:
- Stir in turmeric, ground cinnamon, salt, and pepper. Mix well to coat the meat with the spices.

- Add chopped tomatoes (or canned tomatoes) to the pot. Cook for a few minutes until the tomatoes start to break down.

Incorporate Tomato Paste and Water:
- Dissolve tomato paste in water or beef broth. Pour the mixture into the pot, ensuring that the ingredients are fully covered.
- Bring the stew to a boil, then reduce the heat to low, cover the pot, and let it simmer for about 1.5 to 2 hours or until the meat is tender and the flavors meld.

Add Fried Eggplants:
- Gently add the fried eggplant slices to the stew. Be careful not to break them.
- Cover the pot and let the stew simmer for an additional 30 minutes to allow the flavors to meld further.

Adjust Seasoning:
- Taste the stew and adjust the seasoning if needed. If you prefer a hint of acidity, you can add fresh lime or lemon juice.

Serve:
- Khoresh Bademjan is ready to be served! Garnish with chopped fresh parsley.

This Khoresh Bademjan recipe results in a rich and hearty stew that showcases the wonderful combination of eggplants, meat, and aromatic spices in Persian cuisine. Serve it over steamed rice for a complete and satisfying meal.

Mast O Khiar (Yogurt with Cucumber and Mint)

Ingredients:

- 2 cups Greek yogurt or strained yogurt
- 1 cucumber, peeled, seeded, and finely diced
- 2 tablespoons fresh mint, finely chopped
- 1-2 cloves garlic, minced (optional)
- 1 tablespoon dried rose petals (optional, for garnish)
- Salt and pepper to taste

Instructions:

Prepare the Yogurt:
- If you're using regular yogurt, strain it through a cheesecloth or a fine mesh sieve for a few hours to thicken it. Alternatively, you can use Greek yogurt.

Prepare the Cucumber:
- Peel the cucumber and cut it in half lengthwise. Scoop out the seeds with a spoon. Finely dice the cucumber.

Combine Yogurt and Cucumber:
- In a mixing bowl, combine the strained or Greek yogurt with the diced cucumber.

Add Mint and Garlic:
- Add the finely chopped mint to the yogurt and cucumber mixture. If you like a hint of garlic, you can also add minced garlic at this point.

Season:
- Season the mixture with salt and pepper to taste. Mix everything well to ensure even distribution of flavors.

Chill:
- Cover the bowl and refrigerate the Mast-o-Khiar for at least 30 minutes to allow the flavors to meld and the dish to chill.

Garnish:
- Before serving, you can garnish the Mast-o-Khiar with dried rose petals for a touch of elegance.

Serve:
- Mast-o-Khiar is ready to be served! It can be enjoyed as a side dish, a dip with bread, or as a cooling element alongside spicier Persian dishes.

This simple and refreshing Mast-o-Khiar is a versatile addition to your table, bringing a burst of flavor and a cooling effect to complement a variety of dishes. Adjust the ingredients according to your taste preferences, and enjoy the delightful combination of yogurt, cucumber, and mint.

Kuku Sabzi (Herb Frittata)

Ingredients:

- 2 cups mixed fresh herbs (parsley, cilantro, dill, chives), finely chopped
- 1 cup spinach, finely chopped
- 4 large eggs
- 1 teaspoon baking powder
- 1 tablespoon flour
- 1 cup walnuts, chopped (optional)
- 1 onion, finely chopped
- 2 cloves garlic, minced
- 1 teaspoon turmeric
- Salt and pepper to taste
- Vegetable oil for cooking

Instructions:

Prepare the Herbs:
- Wash and finely chop the fresh herbs (parsley, cilantro, dill, chives) and spinach.

Sauté Onions and Garlic:
- In a pan, sauté finely chopped onions and minced garlic in a bit of vegetable oil until they become translucent.

Mix Herbs and Onions:
- In a large bowl, combine the chopped herbs and spinach with the sautéed onions and garlic.

Prepare the Batter:
- In a separate bowl, beat the eggs. Add baking powder, flour, turmeric, salt, and pepper. Mix well to form a smooth batter.
- Add the egg batter to the bowl of chopped herbs and onions. Mix everything thoroughly.

Optional: Add Walnuts:
- If you like, you can add chopped walnuts to the mixture for added texture and flavor.

Preheat Oven:
- Preheat the oven to 350°F (180°C).

Cook on the Stove:

- In an oven-safe pan, heat some vegetable oil over medium heat.
- Pour the herb and egg mixture into the pan and let it cook for a few minutes on the stove until the edges start to set.

Bake in the Oven:
- Transfer the pan to the preheated oven and bake for about 20-25 minutes or until the Kuku Sabzi is fully cooked and has a golden brown top.

Serve:
- Once cooked, let it cool slightly before slicing. Kuku Sabzi can be served warm or at room temperature.

Enjoy:
- Kuku Sabzi is ready to be enjoyed! It can be served as a side dish, appetizer, or even as a main course.

This Kuku Sabzi recipe is a flavorful and nutritious dish that highlights the vibrant flavors of fresh herbs. It's a wonderful addition to your Persian cuisine repertoire.

Chelo Morgh (Saffron Chicken and Rice)

Ingredients:

For the Chicken Marinade:

- 4 chicken thighs or drumsticks
- 1 cup plain yogurt
- 1 large onion, grated
- 3 cloves garlic, minced
- Juice of 1 lemon
- 1 teaspoon ground saffron threads (soaked in warm water)
- Salt and pepper to taste

For the Rice:

- 2 cups Basmati rice, rinsed and soaked
- 1/2 cup vegetable oil or ghee
- 1/2 teaspoon ground saffron threads (soaked in warm water)
- Salt to taste

For Garnish:

- Sliced almonds or slivered pistachios
- Fresh herbs (parsley, cilantro, or dill)

Instructions:

Marinate the Chicken:
- In a bowl, mix together yogurt, grated onion, minced garlic, lemon juice, soaked saffron (with water), salt, and pepper.
- Coat the chicken pieces with the marinade, ensuring they are well-covered. Allow it to marinate for at least 2 hours, or overnight in the refrigerator for better flavor.

Prepare the Rice:
- In a pot, bring water to a boil. Add salt and the soaked Basmati rice. Cook until the rice is parboiled (half-cooked). Drain the rice.
- In a separate pan, heat vegetable oil or ghee over medium heat. Add a few tablespoons of the parboiled rice and ground saffron mixture, creating a golden crust (tahdig) at the bottom of the pan.

- Layer the remaining parboiled rice over the tahdig. Create a well in the center of the rice with the back of a spoon to allow steam to escape.
- Cover the pot with a clean kitchen towel and a tight-fitting lid. Cook on low heat for about 1.5 to 2 hours to allow the rice to steam and fully cook.

Grill the Chicken:
- Preheat a grill or oven. Grill or roast the marinated chicken until it's fully cooked and has a nice golden color.

Serve:
- Once the rice is fully cooked, gently fluff it with a fork, mixing the layers.
- Arrange the Chelo Morgh on a serving platter. Place the grilled chicken on top of the rice.
- Garnish with sliced almonds or slivered pistachios and fresh herbs.

Enjoy:
- Chelo Morgh is ready to be enjoyed! Serve it with a side of yogurt or a simple salad.

This Chelo Morgh recipe captures the essence of Persian cuisine, offering a delightful combination of saffron-infused rice and flavorful grilled chicken. The crispy tahdig adds an extra layer of texture and flavor to the dish.

Baghali Ghatogh (Lima Bean and Dill Stew)

Ingredients:

- 2 cups fresh or frozen lima beans
- 1 cup fresh dill, chopped
- 3 cloves garlic, minced
- 3 tablespoons vegetable oil
- 1 teaspoon turmeric
- 4 large eggs
- 1 cup Greek yogurt
- Salt and pepper to taste
- Saffron threads (optional, for color)
- Rice for serving

Instructions:

Prepare Lima Beans:
- If using fresh lima beans, shell them. If using frozen, thaw them.

Sauté Garlic and Dill:
- In a pot, sauté minced garlic in vegetable oil until fragrant. Add chopped fresh dill and continue sautéing for a few more minutes.

Add Lima Beans and Turmeric:
- Add lima beans to the pot and stir well. Sprinkle turmeric over the mixture, combining the ingredients.

Cook Lima Beans:
- Add enough water to the pot to cover the lima beans. Simmer until the lima beans are tender. If using fresh lima beans, this may take longer than if using frozen ones.

Prepare Saffron (Optional):
- If using saffron, soak a few saffron threads in warm water and set aside.

Add Greek Yogurt:
- In a bowl, whisk together Greek yogurt and the soaked saffron (if using). Gradually add some of the hot liquid from the pot to the yogurt, whisking continuously to temper it.
- Pour the yogurt mixture back into the pot, stirring well. Let it simmer on low heat.

Poach Eggs:

- Create wells in the stew and gently crack the eggs into these wells. Cover the pot and let the eggs poach until the whites are set but the yolks are still runny.

Season and Serve:
- Season the Baghali Ghatogh with salt and pepper to taste. Adjust the seasoning as needed.
- Serve the Baghali Ghatogh over rice. The eggs and lima beans should be nestled in the flavorful dill and yogurt stew.

Enjoy:
- Baghali Ghatogh is ready to be enjoyed! It's a comforting and aromatic dish with the unique combination of lima beans, dill, and yogurt.

Baghali Ghatogh is often served with rice and is a delightful representation of the rich flavors in Iranian cuisine.

Khoresh Karafs (Celery Stew with Meat)

Ingredients:

- 500g lamb or beef stew meat, cut into cubes
- 1 large onion, finely chopped
- 4 cups celery, sliced into 1-inch pieces
- 1 bunch fresh parsley, chopped
- 1 bunch fresh mint, chopped
- 2 tablespoons vegetable oil
- 2 teaspoons turmeric
- 1 teaspoon cinnamon
- Salt and pepper to taste
- 2 cups water or beef broth
- 2 tablespoons lime or lemon juice (optional, for a hint of acidity)
- 1 tablespoon flour (optional, for thickening)
- Steamed rice for serving

Instructions:

Sauté Onions:
- In a pot, heat vegetable oil over medium heat. Sauté chopped onions until they become golden brown.

Brown the Meat:
- Add the cubed stew meat to the pot. Brown the meat on all sides to seal in the flavors.

Add Spices:
- Stir in turmeric, cinnamon, salt, and pepper. Mix well to coat the meat with the spices.

Cook Celery and Herbs:
- Add sliced celery, chopped parsley, and chopped mint to the pot. Stir to combine the ingredients.

Pour Water or Broth:
- Pour water or beef broth into the pot, ensuring that the ingredients are fully covered.

Simmer:

- Bring the stew to a boil, then reduce the heat to low, cover the pot, and let it simmer for about 1.5 to 2 hours or until the meat is tender and the flavors meld.

Optional Thickening:
- If you prefer a thicker stew, you can mix flour with a bit of water to create a smooth paste. Stir this into the stew and let it simmer for an additional 10-15 minutes.

Adjust Seasoning:
- Taste the stew and adjust the seasoning if needed. If you like a hint of acidity, you can add lime or lemon juice.

Serve:
- Khoresh Karafs is ready to be served! It pairs well with steamed rice.

This Khoresh Karafs recipe results in a comforting stew where the subtle flavors of celery, herbs, and spices complement the tender meat. Enjoy this Persian dish as a hearty and satisfying meal.

Ash-e Doogh (Yogurt Soup)

Ingredients:

- 1 cup barley or rice (pre-soaked if using barley)
- 1 cup chickpeas (pre-soaked if using dried chickpeas)
- 1 large onion, finely chopped
- 4 cups plain yogurt
- 1 cup fresh mint, chopped
- 1 cup fresh cilantro, chopped
- 1 cup fresh dill, chopped
- 2 tablespoons vegetable oil
- 1 teaspoon turmeric
- Salt and pepper to taste
- 4 cups water or vegetable broth
- 1 tablespoon dried mint (for garnish)
- 2 cloves garlic, minced (optional, for garnish)
- 2 tablespoons dried rose petals (optional, for garnish)
- Lime or lemon wedges (for serving)

Instructions:

Prepare Grains and Legumes:
- If using barley, rinse and soak it for a few hours or overnight. If using dried chickpeas, rinse and soak them as well.

Sauté Onions:
- In a large pot, heat vegetable oil over medium heat. Sauté finely chopped onions until golden brown.

Add Turmeric and Herbs:
- Stir in turmeric, chopped mint, cilantro, and dill. Cook for a few minutes until the herbs are fragrant.

Add Barley and Chickpeas:
- Add the pre-soaked barley or rice and chickpeas to the pot. Stir to coat them with the herbs and spices.

Pour Water or Broth:
- Pour water or vegetable broth into the pot, ensuring that the grains and legumes are fully covered. Bring it to a boil.

Simmer:

- Reduce the heat to low, cover the pot, and let it simmer for about 1.5 to 2 hours or until the grains and chickpeas are tender.

Prepare Yogurt Mixture:
- In a bowl, whisk the plain yogurt until smooth. Gradually add some of the hot liquid from the pot to the yogurt, whisking continuously to temper it.
- Pour the yogurt mixture back into the pot, stirring well. Let it simmer on low heat for an additional 15-20 minutes.

Season:
- Season the soup with salt and pepper to taste. Adjust the seasoning as needed.

Garnish:
- In a small pan, heat a bit of oil and sauté minced garlic until golden. Set it aside for garnish.
- Optionally, crush dried mint between your fingers and add it to the soup for garnish. You can also add dried rose petals.

Serve:
- Ash-e Doogh is ready to be served! Ladle the soup into bowls, garnish with sautéed garlic, and serve with lime or lemon wedges on the side.

This Ash-e Doogh recipe results in a nourishing and flavorful yogurt soup that is often enjoyed in Persian cuisine. It's a delightful combination of herbs, grains, and yogurt, creating a unique and comforting dish.

Shishlik (Grilled Lamb Skewers)

Ingredients:

- 2 pounds (about 1 kg) lamb, cut into 1-inch cubes
- 1 large onion, finely grated
- 3 cloves garlic, minced
- 1/4 cup olive oil
- 2 tablespoons plain yogurt
- 2 tablespoons lemon juice
- 1 teaspoon ground cumin
- 1 teaspoon ground coriander
- 1 teaspoon paprika
- 1 teaspoon ground black pepper
- 1 teaspoon salt, or to taste
- Wooden or metal skewers, soaked in water if using wooden ones
- Fresh parsley or cilantro for garnish (optional)

Instructions:

Prepare Marinade:
- In a bowl, combine grated onion, minced garlic, olive oil, yogurt, lemon juice, ground cumin, ground coriander, paprika, black pepper, and salt. Mix well to create the marinade.

Marinate the Lamb:
- Place the lamb cubes in a large bowl or a resealable plastic bag. Pour the marinade over the lamb, ensuring each piece is coated. Massage the marinade into the meat. Cover the bowl or seal the bag and refrigerate for at least 4 hours or overnight for best flavor.

Preheat the Grill:
- Preheat your grill to medium-high heat.

Skewer the Lamb:
- Thread the marinated lamb cubes onto the skewers, leaving a little space between each piece.

Grill the Shishlik:
- Place the skewers on the preheated grill. Grill the lamb for about 10-15 minutes, turning occasionally, until the meat is cooked to your desired doneness and has a nice char on the outside.

Serve:

- Once the Shishlik is cooked, remove it from the grill. Allow it to rest for a few minutes.
- Optionally, garnish with fresh parsley or cilantro before serving.

Enjoy:
- Serve the Shishlik hot with your favorite side dishes or over rice. You can also enjoy it with flatbread and a side of yogurt.

Shishlik is a flavorful and aromatic dish, and the marinade adds a delicious depth of flavor to the tender grilled lamb. It's a great choice for outdoor gatherings and barbecues.

Kalam Polo (Cabbage Rice)

Ingredients:

- 2 cups basmati rice
- 1 small cabbage, finely shredded
- 1 large onion, finely chopped
- 500g ground beef or lamb
- 1/2 cup raisins (optional)
- 1/2 cup dried barberries (zereshk), soaked in water (optional)
- 2 tablespoons tomato paste
- 1 teaspoon ground turmeric
- 1 teaspoon ground cumin
- 1 teaspoon ground coriander
- 1 teaspoon ground cinnamon
- Salt and pepper to taste
- Vegetable oil or butter for cooking
- Saffron threads (optional, for coloring)
- Steamed saffron-infused rice for serving

Instructions:

Prepare the Rice:
- Rinse the basmati rice under cold water until the water runs clear. Soak the rice in water with a bit of salt for about 30 minutes. Then, cook the rice according to your preferred method. You can use a rice cooker or stovetop method.

Sauté Onion and Meat:
- In a large pan, sauté the finely chopped onion in vegetable oil or butter until golden brown. Add the ground beef or lamb and cook until browned.

Add Spices and Tomato Paste:
- Stir in ground turmeric, ground cumin, ground coriander, ground cinnamon, salt, and pepper. Mix well. Add tomato paste and continue cooking for a few more minutes.

Add Cabbage and Raisins:
- Add the finely shredded cabbage to the pan. Mix it well with the meat and spices. If you're using raisins, add them to the mixture.

Simmer:

- Cover the pan and let the mixture simmer over low heat for about 20-30 minutes, or until the cabbage is tender. Stir occasionally to prevent sticking.

Prepare Barberries (Optional):
- If using dried barberries, soak them in water for about 15-20 minutes. Drain before using.

Layering:
- In a separate bowl, mix a portion of the cooked rice with saffron threads (pre-soaked in hot water for color).
- In the serving pot, layer the plain rice, saffron-infused rice, meat and cabbage mixture, and barberries (if using), creating a colorful and flavorful layered dish.

Steam:
- Cover the pot with a lid and place it over low heat for about 20-30 minutes to allow the flavors to meld and the rice to steam.

Serve:
- Once done, gently fluff the rice with a fork. Serve the Kalam Polo on a platter, allowing the layers to be visible.

Enjoy:
- Kalam Polo is ready to be enjoyed! Serve it with yogurt on the side if desired.

Kalam Polo is a savory and aromatic dish that showcases the unique combination of cabbage, spices, and tender meat. It's a comforting and satisfying meal often enjoyed in Persian cuisine.

Mirza Ghasemi (Smoked Eggplant and Tomato Dip)

Ingredients:

- 2 large eggplants
- 4 ripe tomatoes, finely chopped
- 1 large onion, finely chopped
- 4 cloves garlic, minced
- 2 tablespoons vegetable oil
- 1 teaspoon ground turmeric
- 1/2 teaspoon ground cumin
- 1/2 teaspoon paprika
- Salt and pepper to taste
- 3 eggs
- Fresh herbs for garnish (parsley or cilantro)
- Optional: Red pepper flakes for added spice

Instructions:

Smoking the Eggplants:
- Pierce the eggplants in a few places with a fork. Place them directly on a gas stove flame or on a preheated grill. Roast the eggplants, turning occasionally, until the skin is charred and the flesh is soft. Alternatively, you can roast them in the oven at a high temperature.

Peel and Mash Eggplants:
- Let the smoked eggplants cool slightly, then peel off the charred skin. Chop the flesh finely or mash it with a fork. Set aside.

Sauté Onions and Garlic:
- In a pan, heat vegetable oil over medium heat. Add finely chopped onions and sauté until golden brown. Add minced garlic and continue sautéing for a couple of minutes until fragrant.

Add Tomatoes and Spices:
- Add finely chopped tomatoes to the pan. Cook until the tomatoes release their juices and start to break down. Stir in ground turmeric, ground cumin, paprika, salt, and pepper. If you like it spicy, you can add red pepper flakes at this stage.

Combine Eggplant and Tomatoes:

- Add the mashed or finely chopped smoked eggplant to the pan. Mix well with the tomatoes and spices. Let it simmer over low heat for about 15-20 minutes, allowing the flavors to meld.

Create Wells for Eggs:
- Create wells in the mixture using the back of a spoon. Crack an egg into each well.

Cook Eggs:
- Cover the pan and let the eggs cook until the whites are set but the yolks are still runny. You can cook them longer if you prefer well-cooked eggs.

Garnish:
- Garnish the Mirza Ghasemi with fresh herbs such as parsley or cilantro.

Serve:
- Mirza Ghasemi is ready to be served! It is often enjoyed with flatbread or as a side dish.

Mirza Ghasemi is a flavorful and smoky dip that captures the essence of Persian cuisine. It's a versatile dish that can be served as an appetizer or as part of a meal.

Saffron Chicken and Barberry Rice

Ingredients:

For the Chicken:

- 4 chicken thighs or breasts, skin-on
- 1 large onion, finely chopped
- 3 cloves garlic, minced
- 1/4 cup vegetable oil
- 1 teaspoon ground turmeric
- 1 teaspoon ground cumin
- Salt and pepper to taste
- 1/2 cup chicken broth or water

For the Rice:

- 2 cups basmati rice
- 1/4 cup vegetable oil or butter
- 1/2 teaspoon ground saffron threads, dissolved in hot water
- 1 cup barberries (zereshk), soaked in water
- 2 tablespoons sugar
- Salt to taste

Instructions:

For the Chicken:

Marinate the Chicken:
- In a bowl, mix finely chopped onion, minced garlic, ground turmeric, ground cumin, salt, pepper, and vegetable oil. Coat the chicken pieces with this marinade. Let it marinate for at least 1 hour, or preferably overnight in the refrigerator.

Cook the Chicken:
- Heat a pan or skillet over medium-high heat. Add the marinated chicken pieces, and brown them on both sides.

- Once browned, add chicken broth or water to the pan, cover, and let it simmer until the chicken is fully cooked. Ensure the internal temperature of the chicken reaches 165°F (74°C).

For the Rice:

Prepare Basmati Rice:
- Rinse the basmati rice under cold water until the water runs clear. Soak the rice in water with a bit of salt for about 30 minutes. Cook the rice according to your preferred method. You can use a rice cooker or stovetop method.

Prepare Saffron:
- Dissolve ground saffron threads in hot water and mix it with a portion of the cooked rice for coloring.

Prepare Barberries:
- Rinse and soak barberries in water for about 15-20 minutes. Drain them and mix with sugar.

Layer the Rice:
- In a separate pot, layer the cooked rice with the saffron-infused rice, barberries, and a bit of vegetable oil or butter.

Steam the Rice:
- Cover the pot with a lid and let it steam over low heat for about 20-30 minutes to allow the flavors to meld.

Serve:
- Once done, gently fluff the rice with a fork. Serve the Saffron Chicken over the layered rice.

Garnish and Enjoy:
- Optionally, garnish with additional saffron threads or chopped fresh herbs.

Saffron Chicken and Barberry Rice is a festive and flavorful dish in Persian cuisine. The combination of saffron-infused rice, sweet-tart barberries, and tender spiced chicken creates a delicious and visually appealing meal.

Khoresh Mast (Yogurt Stew with Meat)

Ingredients:

- 1 pound (about 500g) beef or lamb stew meat, cut into cubes
- 2 cups plain yogurt
- 1 large onion, finely chopped
- 2 tablespoons vegetable oil
- 2 tablespoons tomato paste
- 1 teaspoon ground turmeric
- 1 teaspoon ground cinnamon
- 1 teaspoon ground nutmeg
- Salt and pepper to taste
- 1 cup chickpeas, cooked (canned or pre-soaked and cooked)
- 2 tablespoons all-purpose flour
- 1 tablespoon dried mint (for garnish)
- Steamed rice for serving

Instructions:

Sauté Onions:
- In a pot, heat vegetable oil over medium heat. Sauté finely chopped onions until they become golden brown.

Brown the Meat:
- Add the cubed stew meat to the pot. Brown the meat on all sides to seal in the flavors.

Add Spices:
- Stir in ground turmeric, ground cinnamon, ground nutmeg, salt, and pepper. Mix well to coat the meat with the spices.

Add Tomato Paste:
- Add tomato paste to the pot and continue stirring for a couple of minutes to incorporate it into the mixture.

Cook Chickpeas:
- If you haven't cooked the chickpeas yet, add them to the pot along with enough water to cover the ingredients. Bring it to a boil, then reduce the heat to low, cover the pot, and let it simmer until the meat is tender.

Prepare Yogurt Mixture:
- In a bowl, whisk the plain yogurt until smooth. Gradually add some of the hot liquid from the pot to the yogurt, whisking continuously to temper it.

- Pour the yogurt mixture back into the pot, stirring well. Let it simmer on low heat for an additional 15-20 minutes.

Prepare Roux (Optional Thickening):

- In a separate pan, make a roux by mixing flour with a bit of water to create a smooth paste. Stir this into the stew and let it simmer for an additional 10-15 minutes if you prefer a thicker consistency.

Adjust Seasoning:

- Taste the stew and adjust the seasoning if needed.

Serve:

- Khoresh Mast is ready to be served! Serve it over steamed rice.

Garnish:

- Just before serving, garnish the Khoresh Mast with dried mint for added flavor.

Khoresh Mast is a rich and comforting stew with the tanginess of yogurt and the warmth of spices. Enjoy this Persian dish with a side of steamed rice for a satisfying meal.

Gondi (Chickpea and Chicken Dumplings)

Ingredients:

For the Dumplings (Gondi):

- 1 cup chickpea flour
- 1 cup ground chicken
- 1 large onion, grated
- 1/2 cup finely chopped fresh herbs (parsley, cilantro, or a combination)
- 1/4 cup vegetable oil or rendered chicken fat
- 1 teaspoon ground turmeric
- 1 teaspoon ground cumin
- 1 teaspoon baking powder
- Salt and pepper to taste

For the Soup:

- 8 cups chicken broth
- 1 large onion, finely chopped
- 3 cloves garlic, minced
- 2 tablespoons vegetable oil
- 1 teaspoon ground turmeric
- Salt and pepper to taste
- Fresh lime or lemon wedges for serving

Instructions:

For the Dumplings (Gondi):

Prepare Dumpling Mixture:
- In a large bowl, combine chickpea flour, ground chicken, grated onion, chopped herbs, vegetable oil or chicken fat, ground turmeric, ground cumin, baking powder, salt, and pepper. Mix well until the ingredients are thoroughly combined.

Form Dumplings:
- Shape the mixture into small, round dumplings, about the size of a walnut.

Boil Dumplings:
- Bring a large pot of salted water to a gentle boil. Carefully drop the dumplings into the boiling water. Cook for about 30 minutes or until the

dumplings float to the surface. Remove them with a slotted spoon and set aside.

For the Soup:

Sauté Onion and Garlic:
- In a separate pot, heat vegetable oil over medium heat. Sauté finely chopped onion and minced garlic until they become golden brown.

Add Turmeric:
- Stir in ground turmeric, salt, and pepper. Cook for an additional minute.

Add Chicken Broth:
- Pour in the chicken broth and bring it to a simmer. Let it simmer for about 10-15 minutes to allow the flavors to meld.

Combine Dumplings and Soup:
- Gently add the boiled dumplings to the soup. Let them simmer together for an additional 10-15 minutes.

Adjust Seasoning:
- Taste the soup and adjust the seasoning if needed. Add more salt or pepper according to your preference.

Serve:
- Ladle the Gondi soup into bowls. Serve hot with fresh lime or lemon wedges on the side.

Gondi is a comforting and flavorful dish, and the dumplings add a unique texture to the soup. Enjoy this traditional Persian recipe as a heartwarming meal.

Lubia Polo (Green Bean Rice)

Ingredients:

- 2 cups basmati rice
- 1 pound (about 500g) green beans, trimmed and chopped
- 1 large onion, finely chopped
- 1 pound ground beef or lamb
- 2 tablespoons tomato paste
- 1 teaspoon ground turmeric
- 1 teaspoon ground cumin
- 1 teaspoon ground cinnamon
- Salt and pepper to taste
- 1/4 cup vegetable oil or butter
- 1/2 cup raisins (optional)
- Slivered almonds or fried onions for garnish (optional)

Instructions:

Prepare Basmati Rice:
- Rinse the basmati rice under cold water until the water runs clear. Soak the rice in water with a bit of salt for about 30 minutes. Cook the rice according to your preferred method. You can use a rice cooker or stovetop method.

Sauté Onions and Meat:
- In a large pan, sauté finely chopped onions in vegetable oil or butter until they become golden brown. Add the ground beef or lamb and cook until browned.

Add Spices and Tomato Paste:
- Stir in ground turmeric, ground cumin, ground cinnamon, salt, and pepper. Mix well. Add tomato paste and continue cooking for a few more minutes.

Cook Green Beans:
- Add the chopped green beans to the pan. Mix them well with the meat and spices. Let them cook for about 5-7 minutes until they start to soften.

Layering:
- In a separate pot, layer the cooked rice with the meat and green bean mixture. Optionally, add raisins between the layers.

Steam the Rice:

- Cover the pot with a lid and let it steam over low heat for about 20-30 minutes to allow the flavors to meld.

Garnish:
- Optionally, garnish Lubia Polo with slivered almonds or fried onions for added flavor and texture.

Serve:
- Once done, gently fluff the rice with a fork. Serve Lubia Polo hot.

Lubia Polo is a fragrant and flavorful dish that combines the earthy taste of green beans with the richness of spiced meat and rice. It's a popular choice in Persian cuisine and makes for a satisfying main course.

Khoresh-e Nokhod (Chickpea Stew)

Ingredients:

- 1 cup dried chickpeas, soaked overnight
- 1 pound (about 500g) lamb or beef stew meat, cut into cubes
- 1 large onion, finely chopped
- 3 cloves garlic, minced
- 2 tablespoons tomato paste
- 1 teaspoon ground turmeric
- 1 teaspoon ground cinnamon
- 1 teaspoon ground cumin
- Salt and pepper to taste
- 1/4 cup vegetable oil
- 2 cups chopped tomatoes (fresh or canned)
- 1 cup chopped fresh herbs (parsley, cilantro, or a combination)
- 1 tablespoon dried lime powder or the juice of 1 lime
- Steamed rice for serving

Instructions:

Soak Chickpeas:
- Place dried chickpeas in a bowl and cover them with water. Let them soak overnight or for at least 8 hours. Drain before using.

Sauté Onions and Meat:
- In a large pot, heat vegetable oil over medium heat. Sauté finely chopped onions until golden brown. Add the stew meat and cook until browned on all sides.

Add Spices:
- Stir in ground turmeric, ground cinnamon, ground cumin, minced garlic, salt, and pepper. Mix well to coat the meat with the spices.

Incorporate Tomato Paste:
- Add tomato paste to the pot and continue stirring for a couple of minutes to incorporate it into the mixture.

Cook Chickpeas:
- Add the soaked and drained chickpeas to the pot. Mix them well with the meat and spices.

Pour Chopped Tomatoes:

- Pour in the chopped tomatoes, and bring the stew to a simmer. Cover the pot and let it cook for about 1.5 to 2 hours or until the meat and chickpeas are tender.

Adjust Seasoning:
- Taste the stew and adjust the seasoning if needed. Add more salt or pepper according to your preference.

Add Fresh Herbs and Lime:
- Stir in the chopped fresh herbs and dried lime powder (or lime juice). Let the stew simmer for an additional 10-15 minutes.

Serve:
- Khoresh-e Nokhod is ready to be served! Serve it over steamed rice.

Khoresh-e Nokhod is a comforting and nutritious stew that showcases the earthy flavors of chickpeas combined with aromatic spices and tender meat. Enjoy this Persian dish as a wholesome main course.

Tahdig with Chicken (Crispy Rice with Chicken)

Ingredients:

For the Rice:

- 2 cups basmati rice
- 4 cups water
- Salt

For the Chicken Mixture:

- 1 pound (about 500g) chicken thighs or breasts, cut into bite-sized pieces
- 1 large onion, finely chopped
- 2 tablespoons vegetable oil
- 2 teaspoons ground turmeric
- Salt and pepper to taste

For the Tahdig (Crispy Rice Layer):

- 1/4 cup vegetable oil or clarified butter (ghee)

Instructions:

Preparing the Rice:

Rinse and Soak Rice:
- Rinse the basmati rice under cold water until the water runs clear. Soak the rice in water with a generous pinch of salt for about 30 minutes.

Boil Rice:
- In a large pot, bring 4 cups of water to a boil. Drain the soaked rice and add it to the boiling water. Cook the rice until it's parboiled (partially cooked), about 6-8 minutes. It should still have a firm bite.

Drain Rice:
- Drain the parboiled rice in a fine-mesh sieve or colander.

Preparing the Chicken Mixture:

Sauté Onions:
- In a separate pot or deep pan, heat vegetable oil over medium heat. Sauté finely chopped onions until golden brown.

Add Chicken:
- Add the chicken pieces to the pot and brown them on all sides.

Season:
- Stir in ground turmeric, salt, and pepper. Mix well to coat the chicken with the spices. Cook until the chicken is fully cooked.

Layering and Creating Tahdig:

Layer Rice and Chicken:
- In the pot with the chicken mixture, layer the partially cooked rice over the chicken.

Create Holes:
- Using the handle of a wooden spoon, create several holes in the rice down to the chicken. This helps steam escape and facilitates the formation of a crispy tahdig.

Add Oil or Ghee:
- Drizzle the vegetable oil or clarified butter (ghee) evenly over the rice.

Steam and Crisp:
- Cover the pot with a lid and place a clean kitchen towel or paper towel between the pot and the lid to absorb excess steam. Cook over low heat for about 30-45 minutes to allow the tahdig to form and the rice to become crispy.

Serve:
- Once the tahdig is crispy and golden brown, gently scoop out the rice and chicken onto a serving platter. Serve the crispy tahdig on the side or on top of the chicken.

Tahdig with Chicken is a delicious and visually appealing dish with the contrast of tender chicken and the crispy layer of rice. It's a favorite in Persian cuisine and is often enjoyed with a side of yogurt or a salad.

Khoresh Bamieh (Okra Stew with Meat)

Ingredients:

- 1 pound (about 500g) okra, washed and trimmed
- 1 pound (about 500g) beef or lamb stew meat, cut into cubes
- 1 large onion, finely chopped
- 2 tablespoons tomato paste
- 3 tablespoons vegetable oil
- 2 cups chopped tomatoes (fresh or canned)
- 1 teaspoon ground turmeric
- 1 teaspoon ground cinnamon
- Salt and pepper to taste
- 1 tablespoon dried lime powder or the juice of 1 lime (optional)
- 2 cups water or beef broth
- Steamed rice for serving

Instructions:

Sauté Onions:
- In a pot, heat vegetable oil over medium heat. Sauté finely chopped onions until they become golden brown.

Brown the Meat:
- Add the cubed stew meat to the pot. Brown the meat on all sides to seal in the flavors.

Add Spices:
- Stir in ground turmeric, ground cinnamon, salt, and pepper. Mix well to coat the meat with the spices.

Incorporate Tomato Paste:
- Add tomato paste to the pot and continue stirring for a couple of minutes to incorporate it into the mixture.

Add Chopped Tomatoes:
- Pour in the chopped tomatoes and cook for an additional 5 minutes until the tomatoes start to break down.

Add Okra:
- Add the washed and trimmed okra to the pot. Mix them well with the meat and tomato mixture.

Pour Water or Broth:

- Pour water or beef broth into the pot, ensuring that the ingredients are fully covered.

Simmer:
- Bring the stew to a boil, then reduce the heat to low, cover the pot, and let it simmer for about 1.5 to 2 hours or until the meat is tender and the flavors meld.

Optional: Add Dried Lime or Lime Juice:
- If desired, add dried lime powder or the juice of 1 lime to the stew for a hint of acidity. Adjust the seasoning to taste.

Serve:
- Khoresh Bamieh is ready to be served! Serve it over steamed rice.

Khoresh Bamieh is a delightful stew that brings together the natural sliminess of okra with the savory richness of meat and spices. Enjoy this Persian dish for a satisfying and comforting meal.

Baqlava (Persian Walnut Pastry)

Ingredients:

For the Filling:

- 2 cups walnuts, finely chopped
- 1/2 cup sugar
- 1 teaspoon ground cinnamon

For the Phyllo Layers:

- 1 pound phyllo dough, thawed if frozen
- 1 cup unsalted butter, melted

For the Syrup:

- 1 cup water
- 1 cup sugar
- 1/2 cup honey
- 1 cinnamon stick
- 3-4 whole cloves
- 1 tablespoon lemon juice

Instructions:

Prepare the Filling:
- In a bowl, combine finely chopped walnuts, sugar, and ground cinnamon. Set aside.

Prepare the Syrup:
- In a saucepan, combine water, sugar, honey, cinnamon stick, cloves, and lemon juice. Bring the mixture to a boil, then reduce the heat and simmer for 10-15 minutes until the syrup thickens slightly. Remove from heat and let it cool. Once cooled, remove the cinnamon stick and cloves.

Assemble the Baqlava:
- Preheat the oven to 350°F (175°C). Brush a baking dish with melted butter.

- Place one sheet of phyllo dough in the bottom of the baking dish and brush it with melted butter. Repeat with several more sheets, layering and buttering each one.
- Sprinkle a portion of the walnut filling evenly over the phyllo layers.
- Continue layering and buttering phyllo sheets, adding more walnut filling in between, until you run out of ingredients. Finish with a top layer of buttered phyllo.

Cut into Diamonds:
- With a sharp knife, carefully cut the layered phyllo and walnut-filled pastry into diamond or square shapes.

Bake:
- Bake in the preheated oven for about 30-40 minutes or until golden brown and crisp.

Pour the Syrup:
- Once out of the oven, immediately pour the cooled syrup over the hot Baqlava, allowing it to soak in and infuse the layers. Ensure that the syrup is evenly distributed.

Cool:
- Allow the Baqlava to cool completely before serving. This helps the layers absorb the syrup and enhances the flavor.

Serve:
- Once cooled, carefully lift the pieces and serve. Baqlava is traditionally enjoyed with tea or coffee.

Baqlava is a sweet and indulgent treat, and its layers of phyllo dough, crunchy nuts, and fragrant syrup make it a popular dessert in Persian cuisine. Enjoy the rich flavors of this delightful pastry!

Mirza Qasemi (Eggplant and Tomato Dip)

Ingredients:

- 2 large eggplants
- 3 medium-sized tomatoes, diced
- 4 cloves garlic, minced
- 1 tablespoon vegetable oil
- 1 teaspoon turmeric
- Salt and pepper to taste
- Fresh parsley for garnish (optional)

Instructions:

Grill the Eggplants:
- Preheat your grill or oven broiler. Pierce the eggplants with a fork to prevent them from bursting. Grill the eggplants until the skin is charred and the flesh is soft. Alternatively, you can roast them in the oven at 400°F (200°C) until tender.

Peel and Mash Eggplants:
- Allow the grilled eggplants to cool slightly. Peel off the charred skin and discard. Mash the softened eggplant flesh with a fork or potato masher until you achieve a smooth consistency.

Sauté Garlic and Tomatoes:
- In a pan, heat vegetable oil over medium heat. Add minced garlic and sauté until fragrant. Add diced tomatoes, turmeric, salt, and pepper. Cook until the tomatoes are soft and the mixture is well combined.

Combine Eggplant and Tomato Mixture:
- Add the mashed eggplant to the pan with the garlic and tomatoes. Mix well, allowing the flavors to meld. Cook for an additional 5-7 minutes.

Adjust Seasoning:
- Taste the mixture and adjust the seasoning if needed. Add more salt or pepper according to your preference.

Garnish and Serve:
- If desired, garnish Mirza Qasemi with fresh chopped parsley. Serve it warm or at room temperature.

Serve with Bread or as a Side:

- Mirza Qasemi is traditionally served with flatbread or pita. It can also be enjoyed as a side dish with rice or as a spread.

Mirza Qasemi is a flavorful and smoky eggplant dip that showcases the rich tastes of Persian cuisine. It's a delightful appetizer or accompaniment to a meal, and its robust flavors are sure to be a hit.

Khoresh-e Albaloo (Sour Cherry Stew with Meat)

Ingredients:

- 1 pound (about 500g) boneless meat (lamb or beef), cut into cubes
- 2 cups fresh or frozen sour cherries, pitted
- 1 large onion, finely chopped
- 2 tablespoons tomato paste
- 1 teaspoon ground turmeric
- 1 teaspoon ground cinnamon
- Salt and pepper to taste
- 2 tablespoons vegetable oil
- 1 cup water
- 1 tablespoon sugar (optional, depending on the tartness of the cherries)
- Fresh herbs for garnish (parsley or cilantro)

Instructions:

Prepare the Meat:
- In a pot, heat vegetable oil over medium heat. Add the chopped onions and sauté until golden brown. Add the meat cubes and brown them on all sides.

Add Spices:
- Stir in ground turmeric, ground cinnamon, salt, and pepper. Mix well to coat the meat with the spices.

Incorporate Tomato Paste:
- Add tomato paste to the pot and continue stirring for a couple of minutes to incorporate it into the mixture.

Add Water and Simmer:
- Pour water into the pot, ensuring that the meat is fully covered. Bring the stew to a boil, then reduce the heat to low, cover the pot, and let it simmer for about 1.5 to 2 hours or until the meat is tender.

Add Sour Cherries:
- Add the pitted sour cherries to the pot. If using fresh cherries, you may want to crush some of them to release their juices. Simmer for an additional 15-20 minutes until the cherries are softened.

Adjust Sweetness (Optional):
- Taste the stew and add sugar if needed. The amount of sugar depends on the tartness of the cherries and your preference for sweetness.

Simmer and Garnish:
- Let the stew simmer for another 10-15 minutes, allowing the flavors to meld. If the stew is too thick, you can add more water to achieve your desired consistency. Garnish with fresh herbs.

Serve:
- Khoresh-e Albaloo is traditionally served with steamed rice. Enjoy the unique combination of sour cherries and savory meat!

Khoresh-e Albaloo is a delightful and tangy Persian stew that captures the essence of Persian cuisine with its blend of sweet and sour flavors. It's a perfect dish to showcase the unique taste of sour cherries.

Maast-o Esfenaj (Yogurt with Spinach)

Ingredients:

- 2 cups plain yogurt
- 1 cup fresh spinach, finely chopped
- 2 cloves garlic, minced
- 1 tablespoon dried mint
- 1 teaspoon salt (adjust to taste)
- 1/2 teaspoon black pepper
- 1 tablespoon olive oil (optional)
- Walnuts for garnish (optional)

Instructions:

Prepare the Spinach:
- Wash the fresh spinach thoroughly and finely chop it. You can blanch the spinach for a minute in boiling water and then drain to enhance color and reduce bitterness, but this step is optional.

Combine Yogurt and Spinach:
- In a mixing bowl, combine the plain yogurt and chopped spinach.

Add Garlic and Seasonings:
- Add minced garlic, dried mint, salt, and black pepper to the yogurt-spinach mixture. Mix well until all the ingredients are evenly incorporated.

Optional: Drizzle Olive Oil:
- For added richness, you can drizzle olive oil over the Maast-o Esfenaj and gently mix it in.

Chill and Serve:
- Refrigerate the Maast-o Esfenaj for at least 1-2 hours before serving. Chilling allows the flavors to meld and enhances the refreshing quality of the dish.

Garnish and Serve:
- Before serving, garnish with crushed walnuts if desired. The walnuts add a nice crunch to the dish.

Serve as a Side:
- Maast-o Esfenaj is typically served as a side dish or accompaniment to main courses. It pairs well with rice dishes, grilled meats, or can be enjoyed with flatbread.

Enjoy:

- Serve this cool and tangy Maast-o Esfenaj as a refreshing addition to your Persian meal.

Maast-o Esfenaj is known for its vibrant green color and the combination of yogurt's creaminess with the freshness of spinach. It's a versatile side dish that adds a burst of flavor to your table.

Kabab Torsh (Sour Chicken Kebabs)

Ingredients:

For the Marinade:

- 1.5 pounds boneless, skinless chicken thighs or breasts, cut into chunks
- 1 cup plain yogurt
- 2 tablespoons pomegranate molasses
- 2 tablespoons olive oil
- 2 cloves garlic, minced
- 1 teaspoon ground turmeric
- 1 teaspoon ground cumin
- 1 teaspoon ground coriander
- Salt and pepper to taste

For the Sauce:

- 1/2 cup pomegranate molasses
- 1/4 cup honey
- 2 tablespoons olive oil
- 1 tablespoon soy sauce
- 2 cloves garlic, minced

Instructions:

Prepare the Marinade:
- In a bowl, combine yogurt, pomegranate molasses, olive oil, minced garlic, ground turmeric, ground cumin, ground coriander, salt, and pepper. Mix well to create the marinade.

Marinate the Chicken:
- Place the chicken chunks in the marinade, ensuring they are well-coated. Cover the bowl and refrigerate for at least 2 hours, or preferably overnight, to allow the flavors to penetrate the chicken.

Thread Chicken onto Skewers:
- Preheat the grill or oven. Thread the marinated chicken chunks onto skewers.

Prepare the Sauce:
- In a small saucepan, combine pomegranate molasses, honey, olive oil, soy sauce, and minced garlic. Heat the mixture over low heat, stirring until well combined. Let it simmer for a few minutes to thicken slightly.

Grill or Oven:
- Grill the chicken skewers over medium-high heat, turning occasionally, until the chicken is cooked through and has a nice char on the edges. Alternatively, you can bake them in the oven at 400°F (200°C) for approximately 20-25 minutes.

Brush with Sauce:
- During the last few minutes of grilling or baking, brush the chicken skewers with the prepared sauce, turning them to ensure even coating.

Serve:
- Once the chicken is fully cooked and glazed with the sauce, remove the skewers from the grill or oven.

Garnish and Enjoy:
- Garnish the Kabab Torsh with additional pomegranate seeds or chopped fresh herbs if desired. Serve the sour chicken kebabs with rice or flatbread.

Kabab Torsh is known for its unique blend of sweet and tangy flavors, making it a delightful and savory dish in Persian cuisine. Enjoy the succulent and juicy chicken skewers with the distinctive taste of pomegranate molasses.

Khoresh-e Beh (Quince Stew with Meat)

Ingredients:

- 1.5 pounds (about 700g) meat (lamb or beef), cut into cubes
- 2 large quinces, peeled, cored, and sliced
- 1 large onion, finely chopped
- 2 tablespoons tomato paste
- 1 teaspoon ground turmeric
- 1 teaspoon ground cinnamon
- Salt and pepper to taste
- Vegetable oil for cooking
- 1 cup water
- 2 tablespoons sugar (optional, depending on the tartness of quinces)
- Fresh herbs for garnish (parsley or cilantro)

Instructions:

Prepare the Quinces:
- Peel, core, and slice the quinces. To prevent them from browning, you can place the slices in a bowl of water with a splash of lemon juice.

Sauté Onions:
- In a pot, heat vegetable oil over medium heat. Sauté chopped onions until golden brown.

Brown the Meat:
- Add the cubed meat to the pot and brown it on all sides.

Add Spices:
- Stir in ground turmeric, ground cinnamon, salt, and pepper. Mix well to coat the meat with the spices.

Incorporate Tomato Paste:
- Add tomato paste to the pot and continue stirring for a couple of minutes to incorporate it into the mixture.

Add Water:
- Pour water into the pot, ensuring that the meat is fully covered. Bring the stew to a boil, then reduce the heat to low, cover the pot, and let it simmer for about 1.5 to 2 hours or until the meat is tender.

Add Quinces:

- Add the sliced quinces to the pot. If using, add sugar to balance the tartness of the quinces. Simmer for an additional 20-30 minutes until the quinces are softened.

Adjust Seasoning:
- Taste the stew and adjust the seasoning if needed. If you prefer a sweeter flavor, you can add more sugar.

Simmer and Garnish:
- Let the stew simmer for another 10-15 minutes, allowing the flavors to meld. Garnish with fresh herbs.

Serve:
- Khoresh-e Beh is traditionally served with steamed rice. Enjoy the delightful combination of savory meat and the distinct flavor of quinces.

Khoresh-e Beh showcases the unique taste of quince in a savory and aromatic stew. The blend of spices and sweetness from the quinces creates a rich and flavorful dish that is a favorite in Persian cuisine.

Ash-e Anar (Pomegranate Soup)

Ingredients:

- 1 cup yellow split peas, rinsed
- 1 cup rice
- 1 large onion, finely chopped
- 2 tablespoons vegetable oil
- 4 cups pomegranate juice (freshly squeezed or store-bought)
- 1/2 cup pomegranate molasses
- 1 tablespoon tomato paste
- 1 teaspoon ground turmeric
- 1 teaspoon ground cumin
- Salt and pepper to taste
- 4 cups water or vegetable broth
- 1 cup fresh herbs (a mix of parsley, cilantro, and dill), chopped
- 1 cup pomegranate arils (seeds) for garnish
- Yogurt for serving (optional)

Instructions:

Cook Split Peas:
- In a pot, combine the rinsed yellow split peas with 4 cups of water. Bring to a boil, then reduce heat and simmer until the split peas are partially cooked (about 20-30 minutes). Drain and set aside.

Sauté Onions:
- In a large pot, heat vegetable oil over medium heat. Add finely chopped onions and sauté until golden brown.

Add Spices:
- Stir in ground turmeric, ground cumin, salt, and pepper. Cook for a couple of minutes until the spices are fragrant.

Add Pomegranate Juice and Molasses:
- Pour in the pomegranate juice, pomegranate molasses, and tomato paste. Mix well to combine the flavors.

Add Cooked Split Peas and Rice:
- Add the partially cooked split peas and rice to the pot. Stir to incorporate them into the pomegranate mixture.

Pour in Water or Broth:

- Add 4 cups of water or vegetable broth to the pot. Bring the soup to a boil, then reduce the heat to low, cover, and simmer until the rice and split peas are fully cooked (about 30-40 minutes).

Adjust Seasoning:
- Taste the soup and adjust the seasoning if needed. Add more salt, pepper, or pomegranate molasses according to your preference.

Add Fresh Herbs:
- Stir in the chopped fresh herbs (parsley, cilantro, and dill) just before serving, reserving some for garnish.

Serve:
- Ladle the Ash-e Anar into bowls. Garnish with fresh herbs and a generous sprinkle of pomegranate arils. Optionally, add a dollop of yogurt on top.

Enjoy:
- Serve this unique and flavorful Pomegranate Soup warm, savoring the combination of tartness from the pomegranates and the richness of the herbs.

Ash-e Anar is a distinctive Persian soup that beautifully blends the tartness of pomegranates with the heartiness of split peas and rice. It's a delicious and comforting dish, especially popular during the fall and winter seasons.

Persian Herb Omelette (Omlet-e Sabzi)

Ingredients:

- 6 large eggs
- 1 cup mixed fresh herbs, finely chopped (parsley, cilantro, dill, green onions)
- 1/2 cup fenugreek leaves (optional), finely chopped
- 1/2 cup leeks or chives, finely chopped
- 1/2 cup spinach, finely chopped
- 1/2 cup feta cheese, crumbled (optional)
- 1 medium onion, finely chopped
- 2 tablespoons olive oil or butter
- Salt and pepper to taste

Instructions:

Prepare the Herbs:
- Wash and finely chop the fresh herbs, fenugreek leaves, leeks, and spinach. If using fenugreek leaves, make sure they are thoroughly cleaned and chopped.

Sauté Onions:
- In a large skillet, heat olive oil or butter over medium heat. Add finely chopped onions and sauté until they become translucent.

Add Herbs:
- Add the chopped fresh herbs, fenugreek leaves, leeks, and spinach to the skillet. Sauté for a few minutes until the herbs are wilted and any excess moisture is evaporated. Remove from heat and let it cool slightly.

Prepare Eggs:
- In a mixing bowl, beat the eggs. Add salt and pepper to taste.

Combine Eggs and Herb Mixture:
- Combine the beaten eggs with the sautéed herb mixture. Mix well to ensure an even distribution of herbs in the eggs.

Cook Omelette:
- Heat the skillet over medium heat. Pour the egg and herb mixture into the skillet. Cook the omelette, lifting the edges with a spatula to allow uncooked eggs to flow underneath.

Optional: Add Feta Cheese:
- If using feta cheese, sprinkle it evenly over one half of the omelette.

Fold and Serve:

- Once the omelette is mostly set but still slightly runny on top, fold it in half using the spatula. Continue cooking for another minute until the eggs are fully set and the cheese (if added) is melted.

Garnish and Serve:
- Slide the Omlet-e Sabzi onto a serving plate. Garnish with additional fresh herbs if desired. Cut into slices and serve hot.

Enjoy:
- This Persian Herb Omelette is commonly enjoyed with flatbread, yogurt, or a side of fresh vegetables.

Omlet-e Sabzi is a delicious and nutritious dish that showcases the vibrant flavors of various herbs. It's a popular choice for a hearty breakfast or brunch in Persian cuisine.

Khoresh-e Havij (Carrot Stew with Meat)

Ingredients:

- 1 pound (about 500g) meat (lamb or beef), cut into cubes
- 4-5 large carrots, peeled and sliced
- 1 large onion, finely chopped
- 2 tablespoons tomato paste
- 1 teaspoon ground turmeric
- 1 teaspoon ground cinnamon
- Salt and pepper to taste
- Vegetable oil for cooking
- 2 cups water or beef broth
- 1 tablespoon lime or lemon juice (optional, for a hint of acidity)
- 2 tablespoons chopped fresh parsley or cilantro (for garnish)
- Steamed rice for serving

Instructions:

Sauté Onions:
- In a pot, heat a few tablespoons of vegetable oil over medium heat. Sauté chopped onions until they become golden brown.

Brown the Meat:
- Add the cubed meat to the pot. Brown the meat on all sides to seal in the flavors.

Add Spices:
- Stir in ground turmeric, ground cinnamon, salt, and pepper. Mix well to coat the meat with the spices.

Add Tomato Paste:
- Add tomato paste to the pot and continue stirring for a couple of minutes to incorporate it into the mixture.

Cook Carrots:
- Add the sliced carrots to the pot and mix with the meat and spices.

Pour Water or Broth:
- Pour water or beef broth into the pot, ensuring that the ingredients are fully covered.

Simmer:

- Bring the stew to a boil, then reduce the heat to low, cover the pot, and let it simmer for about 1.5 to 2 hours or until the meat is tender and the flavors meld.

Adjust Seasoning:
- Taste the stew and adjust the seasoning if needed. If you prefer a hint of acidity, you can add lime or lemon juice.

Garnish:
- Just before serving, garnish the Khoresh-e Havij with chopped fresh parsley or cilantro.

Serve:
- Serve the carrot stew over steamed rice.

Khoresh-e Havij is a comforting and aromatic Persian stew with the sweetness of carrots complementing the savory meat and spices. It's often enjoyed with rice and a side of yogurt.

Mahicheh Stew (Lamb Shank Stew)

Ingredients:

- 4 lamb shanks
- 2 large onions, finely chopped
- 4 carrots, peeled and sliced
- 3 tablespoons tomato paste
- 1 cup split yellow peas, soaked in water for a few hours (optional)
- 2 teaspoons ground turmeric
- 1 teaspoon ground cinnamon
- Salt and pepper to taste
- Vegetable oil for cooking
- 4 cups water or beef broth
- 2 tablespoons lime or lemon juice
- Fresh herbs for garnish (parsley or cilantro)

Instructions:

Prepare Lamb Shanks:
- Rinse the lamb shanks and pat them dry with paper towels. Season with salt, pepper, and ground turmeric.

Sear Lamb Shanks:
- In a large pot, heat vegetable oil over medium-high heat. Sear the lamb shanks on all sides until golden brown. Remove and set aside.

Sauté Onions:
- In the same pot, add chopped onions and sauté until they become golden brown.

Add Tomato Paste:
- Stir in tomato paste and cook for a few minutes until it releases its aroma.

Add Spices:
- Add ground cinnamon, salt, and pepper. Mix well to combine the spices with the onions and tomato paste.

Reintroduce Lamb Shanks:
- Place the seared lamb shanks back into the pot, coating them with the onion and spice mixture.

Add Water or Broth:

- Pour in water or beef broth, ensuring that the lamb shanks are mostly submerged. If using split yellow peas, add them to the pot.

Simmer:
- Bring the stew to a boil, then reduce the heat to low. Cover the pot and let it simmer for about 2 to 2.5 hours or until the lamb is tender. If using split yellow peas, they should be cooked through and soft.

Add Carrots:
- Add the sliced carrots to the pot and continue simmering until they are tender.

Adjust Seasoning:
- Taste the stew and adjust the seasoning if needed. If you prefer a hint of acidity, add lime or lemon juice.

Garnish and Serve:
- Garnish the Mahicheh Stew with fresh herbs such as parsley or cilantro. Serve the stew over steamed rice or with flatbread.

Enjoy:
- This hearty Lamb Shank Stew, Mahicheh, is a comforting and aromatic dish with tender meat and flavorful spices.

Mahicheh Stew is a classic Persian dish that is enjoyed for its rich taste and satisfying texture. The combination of lamb shanks, aromatic spices, and vegetables creates a delicious and wholesome stew.

Gheymeh Nesar (Lentil and Dried Lime Stew)

Ingredients:

- 1 cup yellow split peas, soaked for a few hours
- 1 cup brown or green lentils, rinsed
- 2 large onions, finely chopped
- 3 tablespoons vegetable oil
- 1.5 pounds (about 700g) beef or lamb, cut into cubes
- 2 dried limes (limoo amani), pierced
- 2 tablespoons tomato paste
- 1 teaspoon ground turmeric
- 1 teaspoon ground cinnamon
- Salt and pepper to taste
- 4 cups water or beef broth
- 2 tablespoons lime or lemon juice (optional)
- Fried potatoes for garnish (optional)
- Cooked saffron rice for serving

Instructions:

Prepare Lentils:
- Soak yellow split peas in water for a few hours. Rinse lentils under cold water.

Sauté Onions:
- In a large pot, heat vegetable oil over medium heat. Sauté chopped onions until they become golden brown.

Brown Meat:
- Add the cubed beef or lamb to the pot and brown it on all sides.

Add Spices:
- Stir in ground turmeric, ground cinnamon, salt, and pepper. Mix well to coat the meat with the spices.

Introduce Lentils:
- Add the soaked yellow split peas and rinsed lentils to the pot. Mix with the meat and spices.

Add Tomato Paste:
- Add tomato paste to the pot and continue stirring for a couple of minutes to incorporate it into the mixture.

Pour in Water or Broth:
- Pour water or beef broth into the pot, ensuring that the ingredients are fully covered. Add the pierced dried limes.

Simmer:
- Bring the stew to a boil, then reduce the heat to low, cover the pot, and let it simmer for about 1.5 to 2 hours or until the meat is tender and the lentils are cooked.

Adjust Seasoning:
- Taste the stew and adjust the seasoning if needed. If you prefer a hint of acidity, you can add lime or lemon juice.

Garnish:
- Optionally, fry potato slices until golden brown and use them as a garnish for the stew.

Serve:
- Serve Gheymeh Nesar over cooked saffron rice. The tangy flavor of dried limes adds a distinctive taste to this hearty and comforting Persian stew.

Gheymeh Nesar is a beloved Persian dish that combines the earthy flavors of lentils with the tanginess of dried limes, creating a delicious and satisfying stew. Enjoy it with saffron-infused rice for a complete and flavorful meal.

Persian Rice Pilaf with Pistachios and Dill

Ingredients:

- 2 cups Basmati rice
- 1 large eggplant, peeled and cubed
- 1 cup shelled pistachios
- 1 cup chopped fresh dill
- 1 large onion, finely chopped
- 3 tablespoons vegetable oil
- 1 teaspoon ground saffron (soaked in 2 tablespoons hot water)
- Salt and pepper to taste

Instructions:

Prepare Rice:
- Rinse the Basmati rice under cold water until the water runs clear. Soak the rice in salted water for 1-2 hours. Drain.

Sauté Eggplant:
- In a pan, heat 2 tablespoons of vegetable oil over medium heat. Sauté the cubed eggplant until golden brown. Set aside.

Blanch Pistachios:
- Bring a pot of water to a boil and blanch the pistachios for about 1-2 minutes. Drain and peel the skin off if necessary.

Sauté Onions:
- In a large pot, sauté the finely chopped onions in the remaining vegetable oil until they become golden brown.

Layer the Pot:
- Place a layer of soaked and drained rice at the bottom of the pot. Top it with a layer of sautéed onions, followed by a layer of eggplant, pistachios, and chopped fresh dill. Repeat the layers until all ingredients are used, finishing with a layer of rice on top.

Add Saffron:
- Drizzle the soaked saffron over the top layer of rice.

Steam the Rice:
- Cover the pot with a clean kitchen towel and put the lid on top to create a tight seal. Cook over low heat for about 45-60 minutes. This slow-cooking method will create a crispy golden crust, known as "tahdig," at the bottom of the rice.

Serve:
- Gently fluff the rice with a fork, mixing in the layers. Serve the Persian Rice Pilaf with Pistachios and Dill on a platter, presenting the coveted tahdig on the side or on top.

Enjoy:
- This fragrant and flavorful rice pilaf makes a delicious and elegant side dish, especially popular during Persian celebrations and festive occasions.

Persian Rice Pilaf with Pistachios and Dill is a celebration of flavors and textures, with the pistachios adding a delightful crunch and the dill providing a fresh herbal aroma. Enjoy it as a side dish alongside your favorite Persian main course.

Khoresh-e Karafs (Celery Stew with Meat)

Ingredients:

- 1 pound (about 500g) stewing meat (lamb or beef), cut into cubes
- 1 large onion, finely chopped
- 4-5 celery stalks, sliced into 1-inch pieces
- 1 bunch parsley, finely chopped
- 2 tablespoons vegetable oil
- 2 tablespoons tomato paste
- 1 teaspoon ground turmeric
- 1 teaspoon ground cinnamon
- Salt and pepper to taste
- 2 cups water or beef broth
- 2 tablespoons lime or lemon juice (optional, for a hint of acidity)
- Steamed rice for serving

Instructions:

Sauté Onions:
- In a pot, heat vegetable oil over medium heat. Sauté chopped onions until they become golden brown.

Brown the Meat:
- Add the cubed stewing meat to the pot. Brown the meat on all sides to seal in the flavors.

Add Spices:
- Stir in ground turmeric, ground cinnamon, salt, and pepper. Mix well to coat the meat with the spices.

Add Tomato Paste:
- Add tomato paste to the pot and continue stirring for a couple of minutes to incorporate it into the mixture.

Cook Celery:
- Add the sliced celery to the pot along with chopped parsley. Mix with the meat and spices.

Pour Water or Broth:
- Pour water or beef broth into the pot, ensuring that the ingredients are fully covered.

Simmer:

- Bring the stew to a boil, then reduce the heat to low, cover the pot, and let it simmer for about 1.5 to 2 hours or until the meat is tender and the flavors meld.

Adjust Seasoning:
- Taste the stew and adjust the seasoning if needed. If you prefer a hint of acidity, you can add lime or lemon juice.

Serve:
- Serve Khoresh-e Karafs over steamed rice. The combination of tender meat, aromatic spices, and crisp celery creates a delicious and comforting stew.

Khoresh-e Karafs is a traditional Persian dish that showcases the unique flavor and texture of celery in a savory stew. Enjoy it as a main course with steamed rice for a wholesome and satisfying meal.

Kotlet (Persian Meat Patties)

Ingredients:

- 1 pound (about 500g) ground beef or lamb
- 3 large potatoes, boiled and mashed
- 1 large onion, finely grated
- 2 eggs
- 1 teaspoon turmeric
- 1 teaspoon ground cumin
- Salt and pepper to taste
- Vegetable oil for frying
- Breadcrumbs for coating

Instructions:

Prepare Potatoes:
- Peel, boil, and mash the potatoes. Allow them to cool.

Mix Ingredients:
- In a large mixing bowl, combine the ground meat, mashed potatoes, grated onion, eggs, turmeric, ground cumin, salt, and pepper. Mix the ingredients thoroughly until well combined.

Form Patties:
- Take a portion of the mixture and shape it into a flat, oval patty. The thickness can be adjusted according to your preference.

Coat with Breadcrumbs:
- Coat each patty with breadcrumbs, ensuring an even covering on all sides. Press the breadcrumbs gently onto the surface of the patties.

Fry Kotlet:
- Heat vegetable oil in a pan over medium heat. Fry the patties until they are golden brown on both sides, turning them carefully to maintain their shape. This usually takes about 3-4 minutes per side.

Drain Excess Oil:
- Place the fried Kotlet on a plate lined with paper towels to drain any excess oil.

Serve:
- Serve Kotlet hot as a main dish. It can be accompanied by rice, bread, or a side of salad.

Enjoy:
- Enjoy these crispy and flavorful Persian Meat Patties, Kotlet, with your favorite condiments or dipping sauces.

Kotlet is a beloved Iranian dish, often served during family gatherings and special occasions. The combination of ground meat, mashed potatoes, and aromatic spices creates a delicious and satisfying meal.

Sabzi Khordan (Fresh Herb Platter)

Ingredients:

- Fresh herbs (a combination of mint, parsley, cilantro, tarragon, and dill)
- Radishes, washed and sliced
- Scallions, washed and sliced
- Feta cheese, crumbled (optional)
- Lavash or flatbread for serving

Instructions:

Prepare Fresh Herbs:
- Wash and dry the fresh herbs thoroughly. Chop them finely or leave them as whole sprigs, depending on your preference.

Arrange on a Platter:
- Arrange the fresh herbs on a serving platter. Create small bundles or piles of each herb variety.

Add Radishes and Scallions:
- Place sliced radishes and scallions on the platter alongside the fresh herbs.

Include Feta Cheese (Optional):
- If you like, crumble feta cheese and add it to the platter for an extra layer of flavor and texture.

Serve with Lavash or Flatbread:
- Serve Sabzi Khordan with pieces of lavash or flatbread. Traditionally, people take a piece of flatbread, grab some herbs, radishes, and cheese, and create a bite-sized wrap.

Enjoy:
- Sabzi Khordan is often enjoyed as a refreshing and palate-cleansing side dish. It complements a wide range of Persian dishes and adds a burst of freshness to the meal.

Variations:
- You can customize your Sabzi Khordan by adding other fresh herbs like basil or chives. Some variations may include walnuts, sliced cucumbers, or even a squeeze of lime or lemon juice for extra zing.

Sabzi Khordan is not only a delightful accompaniment to Persian meals but also a healthy and vibrant way to enjoy a variety of fresh herbs. It adds a burst of color and flavor to the dining table.

Khoresh-e Fesenjan (Pomegranate Walnut Stew with Chicken)

Ingredients:

- 1 whole chicken, cut into pieces (or use chicken thighs or breasts)
- 2 cups walnuts, finely ground
- 2 cups pomegranate molasses (or concentrate)
- 1 large onion, finely chopped
- 2 tablespoons vegetable oil
- 1 teaspoon ground cinnamon
- 1 teaspoon ground turmeric
- Salt and pepper to taste
- 2 tablespoons sugar (optional, adjust to taste)
- Pomegranate seeds for garnish (optional)

Instructions:

Prepare Chicken:
- In a large pot, heat vegetable oil over medium heat. Sauté the chopped onion until golden brown. Add the chicken pieces and brown them on all sides.

Add Spices:
- Stir in ground cinnamon, ground turmeric, salt, and pepper. Mix well to coat the chicken with the spices.

Ground Walnuts:
- Add the finely ground walnuts to the pot. Stir continuously over medium heat for about 5-7 minutes until the oils in the walnuts start to release.

Pomegranate Molasses:
- Pour in the pomegranate molasses (or concentrate). Mix well to combine all the ingredients.

Simmer:
- Bring the stew to a gentle boil, then reduce the heat to low, cover the pot, and let it simmer for about 2 to 2.5 hours. Stir occasionally to prevent sticking.

Adjust Sweetness:
- Taste the stew and adjust the sweetness by adding sugar if needed. The level of sweetness can vary based on personal preference.

Check Chicken:

- Ensure the chicken is tender and cooked through. The stew should have a thick and rich consistency.

Serve:
- Serve Khoresh-e Fesenjan over a bed of Persian rice (Chelow) or steamed basmati rice. Garnish with pomegranate seeds for a festive touch.

Enjoy:
- This Pomegranate Walnut Stew is a delightful blend of savory and sweet flavors. It's a comforting and luxurious dish often enjoyed during special occasions and celebrations.

Khoresh-e Fesenjan is a unique and flavorful dish that showcases the delicious combination of pomegranate and walnuts. The result is a luscious and aromatic stew that is sure to be a hit at your dining table.

Sirabi Polo (Cherry Rice)

Ingredients:

- 2 cups Basmati rice
- 2 cups fresh or frozen cherries, pitted
- 1 cup slivered almonds or chopped pistachios
- 1 large onion, finely chopped
- 3 tablespoons butter or vegetable oil
- 1 teaspoon ground cinnamon
- 1/2 teaspoon ground cardamom
- 1/2 teaspoon ground cumin
- Salt to taste
- 2 tablespoons sugar (optional, adjust to taste)
- 1/4 cup rose water (optional, for added fragrance)

Instructions:

Prepare Rice:
- Rinse the Basmati rice under cold water until the water runs clear. Soak the rice in salted water for 1-2 hours. Drain.

Sauté Onions:
- In a large pot, heat butter or vegetable oil over medium heat. Sauté the chopped onion until golden brown.

Add Spices:
- Stir in ground cinnamon, ground cardamom, ground cumin, and salt. Mix well to coat the onions with the spices.

Add Cherries and Sugar:
- Add the pitted cherries to the pot. If the cherries are tart, you can add sugar to balance the sweetness. Stir gently to combine.

Prepare Rice Layers:
- In a separate pot, parboil the soaked and drained rice in salted water for about 5-7 minutes until it's slightly cooked but still firm. Drain the rice.

Layer the Pot:
- Layer the partially cooked rice over the cherry mixture in the pot. Sprinkle slivered almonds or chopped pistachios on top.

Steam the Rice:
- Create a well in the center of the rice, cover the pot with a clean kitchen towel, and put the lid on top to create a tight seal. Cook over low heat for

about 45-60 minutes. This slow-cooking method will create a crispy golden crust, known as "tahdig," at the bottom of the rice.

Add Rose Water (Optional):
- If using rose water, drizzle it over the rice just before serving for added fragrance.

Serve:
- Gently fluff the rice with a fork, mixing in the layers. Serve Sirabi Polo hot, presenting the tahdig on the side or on top.

Enjoy:
- Sirabi Polo is a flavorful and festive dish that makes a wonderful side or main course, especially during celebrations and special occasions.

Sirabi Polo is a beautiful and aromatic dish that captures the essence of Persian cuisine with its unique blend of sweet cherries, aromatic spices, and crispy tahdig. Enjoy it with your favorite Persian main courses or as a centerpiece during festive gatherings.

Ash-e Reshteh (Noodle and Herb Soup)

Ingredients:

- 1 cup lentils, rinsed and drained
- 1 cup chickpeas, soaked overnight and drained
- 1 cup red kidney beans, soaked overnight and drained
- 1 large onion, chopped
- 3 cloves garlic, minced
- 1 cup chopped leeks (optional)
- 1 cup chopped green onions
- 1 cup chopped cilantro
- 1 cup chopped parsley
- 1 cup chopped spinach
- 1 cup chopped dill
- 1 cup chopped chives
- 1/2 cup vegetable oil
- 1 cup reshteh (Persian noodles) or linguine, broken into small pieces
- 2 tablespoons all-purpose flour
- 1/2 cup Kashk (liquid whey, optional)
- Salt and pepper to taste
- 1 teaspoon ground turmeric
- 1 tablespoon dried mint for garnish
- 4 cups water
- 8 cups vegetable or chicken broth

Instructions:

Prepare Legumes:
- In a large pot, combine lentils, chickpeas, and kidney beans with 4 cups of water. Bring to a boil, then reduce heat and simmer until the legumes are tender.

Sauté Onion and Garlic:
- In a separate pan, sauté chopped onions in vegetable oil until golden brown. Add minced garlic and continue to sauté until fragrant.

Add Flour and Turmeric:
- Sprinkle flour and turmeric over the sautéed onions and garlic. Stir well to combine and cook for a few minutes to remove the raw taste of the flour.

Add Noodles:

- Add broken reshteh or linguine to the pot. Stir to coat the noodles with the onion and flour mixture.

Add Herbs:
- Add chopped leeks, green onions, cilantro, parsley, spinach, dill, and chives to the pot. Mix well to combine.

Add Broth:
- Pour in the vegetable or chicken broth, then add the cooked legumes. Season with salt and pepper to taste.

Simmer:
- Simmer the soup over medium heat for about 45 minutes to an hour, or until the noodles and legumes are fully cooked.

Add Kashk (Optional):
- If using Kashk (liquid whey), add it to the soup and stir well. Adjust the seasoning if needed.

Serve:
- Ladle the Ash-e Reshteh into bowls. Garnish each serving with a sprinkle of dried mint.

Enjoy:
- This nourishing and comforting Ash-e Reshteh is best enjoyed hot. Serve it with a squeeze of lime or lemon if desired.

Ash-e Reshteh is often served during special occasions and celebrations, and its rich combination of legumes, herbs, and noodles makes it a wholesome and satisfying dish.

www.ingramcontent.com/pod-product-compliance
Lightning Source LLC
LaVergne TN
LVHW081601060526
838201LV00054B/2004